Norrie's T

G000273052

This is the autobiography of a remarkable lady who is the last surviving member of author Thomas Hardy's 'Hardy Players' of the 1920s. She was born Augusta Noreen Bugler and is now Norrie Woodhall, Norrie to her friends and still Gus to her family.

'Norrie's Tale' gives an account of life in the family hotel in Dorchester where she was born at the beginning of the twentieth century, and of her's and her sister Gertrude's part in Hardy's plays at that time.

Norrie lived her first thirty or so years in Dorchester and then in the 1930s moved to the country a few miles east of Dorchester. She played her part in the war effort as the keeper of a poultry farm supplying the locally stationed Forces, as well as being an Air Raid Precautions warden.

Norrie married late and those 25 years were to be the happiest of her life. Now a widow, and having been through the traumatic experiences of ill health, both her own and that of close family members, she is a beacon of strength to be admired.

Norrie celebrated her one hundredth birthday in December 2005.

Acknowledgements and a dedication by the Author

When I was first encouraged by my friends Olive Blackburn and Devina Symes to write my memoirs I had no idea how much I would come to learn about my own family. Derek Bugler, Petrina and Peter Stevens, Kay Kearsey, Jean West and Hilda Parsons all presented me with the results of their research, for which I am most grateful.

In addition, I would like to express my sincere appreciation for all that Alan Hodge has done to bring the book to publication. In particular his photographic skills have helped greatly to illustrate the period of my life.

I dedicate this book to my late husband Frank Woodhall with whom I spent the happiest years of my life.

Picture credits

Cover picture: By courtesy of the Trustees of Max Gate, Dorchester.
Figs. 4, 9, 10, 11, 31, 34: By courtesy of The Dorset Natural History and Archaeological Society.
Figs. 2, 6, 8, 13, 14, 16, 17, 22, 23, 24, 25, 28, 35: A N Woodhall.
Figs. 18, 19, 20, 21, 29, 30: Alan Hodge.
Figs. 32, 33: Doreen Hodge.
Fig. 26: Hartmut Paulus.
Figs. 1, 3, 5, 7, 12, 15, 27: unattributable.

General Information

Printed and bound by **Creeds the Printers**, Broadoak, Bridport, DT6 5NL

This is a **Lullworde Publication**, first published in Great Britain in 2006.
Lullworde Publications, Seavale, Lulworth Cove, Wareham, BH20 5RJ

ISBN: 0-9504053-4-5
         978-0-9504053-4-6

All the profits from the sales of this book will go to
Dorset cancer care and relief charities.

CONTENTS

Part Five: Illness and Recovery

Part Six: A New Millennium

Part Seven: Up-to-date – 2005

Norrie's Tale . . .

The Last of the Hardy Players

Part One: Childhood

1.1 Early days in Dorchester

I was born Augusta Noreen Bugler (still 'Gus' to my family) in Dorchester in 1905 at the Central Temperance Hotel. I had three older siblings, Gertrude, Eileen and Arthur.

In 1922, when I was 16 years of age, I sat at a table in the hotel, then my home, looking at a blank page of writing paper. No inspiration came. The paper remained blank, no story was written. I had no experience of life then. I had just left school, the Grammar School at Beaminster where I had gained a certificate enabling me to continue my education at a College. That was not to be. Why? An older sister who loved business life, suddenly decided to get married and my mother begged me to take her place, working in the hotel. Very reluctantly I was made to do so. I did not like this arrangement, varied as it proved to be, keeping accounts, dressing display windows, serving customers which I hated; some could be very, very tiresome!

Now that I have reached my 100th birthday, I again sit in front of a table in my home at Owermoigne; this time the paper will no longer remain blank – with a whole lifetime behind me, and two World Wars, both bringing despair and resignation over the long years.

Fig. 1   The Central Temperance Hotel and Dining Rooms, South Street, Dorchester, 1910s

1.2 The 'Central'

The Central Temperance Hotel was a grey stone building built in 1896. It stood next to the General Post Office in South Street. When I was a child I used to hear the officials in the Post Office stamping each letter and postcard by hand 'till I fell asleep. I still have post cards with halfpenny stamps on the back. The hotel itself, which all knew as the 'Central' was built on the lower level of the property. The hotel and restaurant in the days before the Great War of 1914-18 relied on servants, as they were then called, to help run the business. The cost of labour then was very little by modern standards. Some of the servants slept in the hotel. Usually their homes were in the nearby villages.

My mother had a wonderful business ability. She was in charge of the hotel, shop and restaurant. My father, a rather shy retiring man, ran the bake-house. Bread, cakes of every description, wedding and Christmas cakes a speciality, were all made on the premises. The recipes were rather different then, tastier than the produce of today. In the bake-house there were wooden bins where bread was made manually. Above the bake-house there was a loft. Flour was delivered in 2 $1/2$ cwt. sacks which were hauled up to the loft from a horse-pulled dray by means of a pulley. Coconut in boxes was stored too. I knew where it was. I climbed up the upright ladder connecting the bake-house to the loft, quite a stretch for my little short legs, then spent hours by myself in the warm atmosphere, watching the cockroaches run around or helping myself to the coconut, should a case be open.

On Sundays the shop was shut, as were all businesses in Dorchester. After morning service those who attended came home to a welcome sight – Sunday roast, which consisted of locally grown vegetables together with a large joint of very fatty meat surrounded by roast potatoes. I watched my father carving the meat, placing the slices on the plates as fast as he could, then passing the plate to my mother who served the vegetables also as fast as she could so that we should eat a hot meal. After this a pudding or tart would be served with custard; and eventually a cup of tea.

Only gas light was available then. Gas mantles, very delicate in texture and difficult to adjust, gave a whitish light at night. Coal fires were in the house and the commercial room on the second floor, and coke fires adjacent to the ovens in the bake-house. Knives were cleaned after use on a special board kept in the scullery. Eggs were individually tested before being stored in a lime solution. At that time eggs were only laid in the spring.

Sheets, blankets etc. were washed by hand in the yard on a level with the kitchen, then folded through the rollers of a heavy mangle. Ironing was done on a large kitchen table, also used by the servants for meals. Cutlery and hardware were all washed and dried by hand. That was part of the world of heavy work which the workers of 1914-18 war, and before that, endured.

Food for the whole community was mainly purchased from the weekly Wednesday market. Milk was delivered daily from a specially constructed dray containing large milk containers with covers. A ladle was used to give correct amounts – all this very early in the morning. During the long winter nights some of the servants – friends rather than servants – would join my parents in the living room. Sheets, blankets etc. requiring repairs were mended by means of a hand operated sewing machine.

It was in the dining room next to the living room where Thomas Hardy would come at times to be with the Hardy Players to help and advise. Rehearsals fascinated me. There was a thick heavy curtain hanging between the glass doors of the living and dining rooms. I found a convenient hole in that curtain. So I watched through the years *The Woodlanders*, *The Mellstock Quire*, *Return of the Native* and *Desperate Remedies* until I was old enough to be a Hardy Player myself.

In the early days of the Central there was no hot or cold water system in the hotel. Cold water would be in each bedroom in a decorated jug and basin on a wash stand. Each morning a housemaid had to travel up several flights of stairs with the jugs of hot water, boiled in the kitchen, to be placed outside each bedroom door with the words "Your hot water, Sir".

Commercial travellers were the main source of the hotel's revenue. They would book a room for several days during which they visited the various shops in the town for orders. The goods were brought by rail from firms such as Cadbury to Dorchester. Then a horse-drawn covered vehicle was driven around to the shops delivering the orders. The shops in those days were owned mostly by Dorset people who lived above their premises.

Early during the Great War troops were billeted in the Central. Unbeknown to my parents, I would climb up a number of steps to the top of the hotel where I could hear a soldier playing a violin behind a closed door. He was the brother of Albert Salmons, a very gifted professional violinist of those days. They both survived that dreadful war.

Facing South Street were central doors, each side of which were large display windows set in light oak fittings, and a door to give access to the hotel. Above, on a light green background protected by glass were the words 'Confectioner. AH Bugler. Restauranteur'. Above this was the hotel. The shop, in which several dining tables could be placed if necessary, gave access to the family living room and the public dining room and the nearby kitchen and store rooms. The dining room had a corrugated iron roof and overhead glass fittings to give light and ventilation. A heavy rainfall meant that customers had great difficult regarding hearing each others' conversation.

In front of the kitchen window was a small yard, above which was the second level of the property – about ten feet above. On this level was the bake-house, garage and several storage sheds with access to Trinity Street. One shed contained live rabbits, aiding food shortage during the First World War. About 12 stone steps also connected the two levels. As a small child I fell down these without hurting myself, but frightened my mother when I fell down the opening in front of the kitchen window. The doctor was hurriedly sent for. I do not remember the fall which could have killed me had I not instinctively raised my little hands to my head, but I do remember hearing the doctor's footsteps coming nearer and nearer along the passage leading to the bedroom door, the opening of the door and his gruff voice saying, "Where is she? Can't be much the matter if we can't find her." I was under the bed out of his way for I was terrified as he was so tall and abrupt in speech.

1.3 More early memories

When I was about five years old I was invited to a party which was held in a hall with a stage in Dorchester. Someone said "Is there any one able to sing or recite here?" I shouted out "I can" and joyfully I went up onto the stage. This is what I sang:

> *"Has anyone seen my tiddler?*
> *Tiddle iddle iddle iddle iddler.*
> *I caught a little fish on a cotton and a pin.*
> *Oh how I laughed when I dragged him in.*
> *But coming home, oh dear oh,*
> *A rude boy, Dickie Diddler*
> *Put his finger in my galley pot*
> *And pinched my tiddler!*
> *Tiddler iddle iddle iddle iddler."*

I continued the last line over and over again at the top of my voice till I was quite forcibly removed from the stage. I enjoyed it but I've a feeling that maybe my audience was not amused.

I did not attend school until I was about seven years of age, around 1912. Perhaps my grandfather was responsible for this for he would tell my parents that I was not growing very fast compared to my two sisters. In fact he plainly insinuated that he did not think my parents would be able to 'rear' me. The companionship of his little grandchild was yet another reason he loved children. So I was kept at home longer because I was supposed to be delicate. My two sisters and brother, all much older than me, often teased me regarding my size calling me a 'nestle tripe' as well as other names. This tended to create an inferiority complex over the years. There was another boy more my age. He would have been my playmate. He died in infancy. My mother used to say he was fair-haired just like me. The rest of the family had dark hair.

1.4 A naughty little girl

I still have, even to this day, a rather dilapidated post card album which somehow survived the changing of homes over the years. There are many quite beautiful cards, in colour, of the days before the war of 1914. Many are birthday cards showing horses – black, white, brown ones. Everyone knew I loved horses. A few of the cards with wording seem quite funny, depicting the humour of those days.

This album also preserved a very small photograph of myself when about five years old. This photograph has faded over the years. My much loved chicken, whom I called 'Little', is closely clasped in my arms. In the background is an old wall, now demolished. It was just outside my parent's property in Trinity Street, Dorchester. At that age I was rather a lonely little girl. I did not want to play with dolls. Horses and chickens were my favourite companions. I had to be content with toy horses, whilst a real live chicken gave me lots of fun and happiness.

One abnormally hot sunny day Little, it seemed to a five-year-old, was far too hot as she held her wing feathers away from her body to try to cool herself, and her beak was opened wide gasping for air. So I plucked her feathers leaving only the wing and tail feathers, probably because they were too difficult to remove. Little appeared to be hardly better for the treatment and seemed to be very distressed and shivering having hardly any feathers left on her body. In one of the nearby sheds was a bucket of tar and a brush that was kept for preserving the corrugated roofs of the various sheds and a dining room. That, my five year old mind reasoned, was just what I wanted. The tar could be the means of restoring the feathers to where they once were. Little staggered about the yard dripping tar and feathers, a really miserable poor little chicken.

A commercial traveller hoping for an order came into the

Fig. 2 Myself when I was five with my pet chicken 'Little', 1911

yard from Trinity Street to see my father who was in the bake-house. The traveller's eyes alighted on something he had never seen before – or since. He saw Little tarred and feathered trying to walk. "Good God Mr. Bugler, what is that?" were his first words to father. Little was caught, carried down the stone steps to the scullery where my mother tried to remove the tar which proved impossible. Thus it was that the demise of Little took place much earlier than it should have done.

One of the servants, who was an ardent Roman Catholic scolded me severely saying "Oh! you naughty little girl. What will Jesus say when he knows what you have done?" "He won't know" I replied. "I was in the coal house; it's ever so dark in there, no one could see me". The photograph of Little has, by means of the wonderful advancement of photography of later years, been restored.

When I was very small we had a collie dog called Ben. I used to pretend he was a horse. With my legs just touching the ground I imagined myself on Black Bess riding to York, until Ben sat down and I rolled off his back. I taught Ben to 'tiddle-tail'. He would chase around and around after his tail until he probably felt quite dizzy.

My mother used to go by train to Southampton to see her sister. She promised me a 'gee-gee', my name for a toy horse. She had bought me a little blue coat and she was longing to see if it was the right size. I was very naughty; I wouldn't let her put on my coat until I had seen my toy horse and cart.

I loved to go to Cedar Park Villas to be with my much-loved grandfather. At one period he had someone I knew as auntie Gertie looking after him. Out of the kindness of his heart he had given the little-known relative from London a home, little knowing that she was an alcoholic. I was playing by myself in the small garden at the back of the house when I noticed under a bush some bottles. I wondered whether grandfather knew anything about them so I took one of them for him to see. He knew what that bottle was although he was a teetotaller himself. Auntie Gertie was quickly despatched back to London after a hastily called family discussion. An alcoholic was not a suitable person to look after an old man.

Grandfather loved having me with him. On one occasion my cousin Marjory was invited as well. I rather imagined that this had not met with auntie Gertie's approval. Grandfather had made one of his gorgeous apple tarts, the pastry of which was made from butter. I shall never forget the crispness of that pastry – there's nothing like it today. We had already had one helping of this apple tart but we would have loved to have a second helping. So we gazed longingly at it to no effect. Auntie Gertie did not like children so we could not summon up enough courage to ask. Grandfather died in 1918 just after the first World War.

Fig. 3   Henry Bugler, my much-loved grandfather, circa 1912

1.5 To school

In those days all children walked to school. It was a safe world to be living in. I used to walk by myself from my home in South Street, up the steep incline past the General Post Office in New Street, into Trinity Street until I reached the entrance to Bowling Alley Walks – one of the lovely avenues of trees which then surrounded Dorchester – along the gravel path underneath this avenue of trees until a small gate was reached which gave access to the Borough Gardens, then surrounded by iron railings which were removed for use in the 1939 war. I continued through the Gardens, passing the tennis courts, past the Jubilee Clock to reach the large iron gates facing Cornwall Road. Then over the road to enter Casterbridge School. The building is still there though no longer a school.

A father and daughter were responsible for the school for boys and girls. A cane was used to punish unruly boys, the girls being kept in after school hours to write 'lines' if punishment should be necessary. There was a slow burning 'combustion' stove to heat the classroom. The words "slow but sure combustion" were engraved on the circular cover of this form of heating. Basil Walne, feeling very cold one winter morning, sat on this stove a little longer than he should have done. When he hastily rose the word "slow" could be plainly seen on the seat of his trousers! Of course the rest of the class thought this very funny, certainly applicable to Basil. At his age he had no wish to learn and was always the boy to be in trouble, for which he became familiar with cane punishment. 'Lott and Walne' were for many years in business in Dorchester.

School plays were produced at the end of the winter term at the Corn Exchange in Dorchester. When the *Pied Piper of Hamelin* was produced by the school a number of small girls were dressed as rats – complete with tails. To give the appearance of a horde of rats they had to cross the stage, run around the back of the scenery and onto the stage again several times. Little Norah Godwin was one of the rats. Each time she came on to the stage she stopped to look out at the audience to see if she could see her parents. After about the third time that this happened the audience became quite overcome with laughter.

Norah's parents owned and lived above their shop containing very beautiful china of every description. This shop faced High West Street, partly in Trinity Street where the Georgian theatre is still discernable. Part of Maeterlinck's *Blue Bird* was performed on one of these school play occasions. Olive and Phyllis Templeman were at the school for a short while. At that time Phyllis had difficulties with pronunciation. She was cast as Father Time, the wording was "where is he whose hour has come". Again and again she would say "where is 'ee 'oo's hower 'as come". Nothing could persuade her to say her sentence correctly. Eventually the teacher had to change it to "are ye ready?"

The very old premises belonging to the Templeman family, selling leather goods and clothing, has quite recently (2004) changed hands. The shop stands in South Street on the corner of Durngate Street. For years it remained part of the Dorchester of my youth.

It was at these school plays that we used to see Mr. Tilley who was the stage manager. He loved children. He used to stand in the stage wings pulling the funniest of faces to amuse them. We all loved Mr. Tilley.

When Shakespeare's *As You Like It* was performed around 1912 Mr. Tilley noticed that my sister Gertrude gave a quite unusual performance as an old man. She was still at Casterbridge School then. This performance eventually resulted in her first appearance as one of the Hardy Players at sixteen years of age. The year 1913 saw the production of *The Woodlanders* by Thomas Hardy, at the Dorchester Corn Exchange. Gertrude, as Marty South, spoke the last sentence of the play. She knelt near the 'dead' body of Giles Winterborne, the man the young girl had so loved, repeating the exact words of the book:

> 'Now, my own own love, you are mine and on'y mine; for she has forgot 'ee at last, although for her you died. But I – whenever I get up I'll think of 'ee, and wherever I lie down I'll think of 'ee. Whenever I plant the young larches I'll think that none can plant as you planted; and whenever I split a gad and whenever I turn the cider wring, I'll say none could do it like you. If ever I forget your name let me forget home and heaven . . . But no, no, my love, I never can forget 'ee; for you was a _good_ man, and did good things!'

————

The curtain descended, the audience was silent for a while. Then prolonged clapping – at every performance.

During the war years of 1914 to 1918 the Hardy Players ceased – with one exception. Scenes from *The Dynasts* were given one year. Thomas Hardy wrote in the part of a serving maid for my sister Gertrude. I have memories of hearing her sing *My Love's Gone a'Fighting Where War Trumpets Sound*. The war brought about the formation of 'The Gypsies'.

1.6 Brother Arthur & cousin Marjory

My brother Arthur (his nick-name was Sonnie) was about nine years older than me. He was old enough to join the army near the end of the war. He was sent to France to drive lorries. I have a picture card album which has survived all these years. In it are several cards from France sent by him. They are beautiful; the embroidery on them has retained colour owing to their being kept in the dark. My brother was invalided out of the army suffering from tuberculosis. Starting army lorries was very heavy going. When cold, the lorry would not start despite much winding by the driver. The starting handle was in front of the lorry and could sometimes be responsible for an injured back or arm. In my brother's case it was his back. Fresh air was supposed to be the cure for tuberculosis then. Of that he had plenty, day and night, for he was sent to a Broadmayne farm where a tent was erected for him and a qualified nurse provided to look after him. He did not enjoy this at all. She was a very strict nurse and he certainly had to do what he was told. He had to rest on his back as much as possible. I used to cycle over to Broadmayne to see him. Often he had another visitor, but she died of the same illness. He told me once that a cow came to his bed and tried to lick his face, which caused it to go green in places. I never found out if this was true as he had a habit of pulling my leg.

My cousin, Marjory Brown, was the one relative near my age. She lived near the barracks then. When I visited her I loved to listen to the soldiers drilling in the barrack square. The sergeant's voice could have been heard a mile away! When Marjory recovered from her ordeal of living in a wooden hut by herself for two years, the then supposed cure for tuberculosis, life became rather complicated for me. A cousin, whom I did not know, visited her every Saturday. I was not invited; thus I lost Marjory's companionship. Her mother too became difficult, religion causing a great deal of stress.

1.7 'The Gypsies'

Early in the 1914-18 war some of the Hardy Players formed a concert party which they called 'The Gypsies'. All proceeds were given to war charities. I truly enjoyed rehearsing after school hours. Dressed as a boy I would strut across the stage as Burlington Bertie with a monocle held in one eye and a cane held in one hand. Even my grandfather Bugler thought I was a boy when I was taken to see him.

A short poem called *The Night Wind* became hilarious on one occasion. Our announcer – there were no programmes as such – pompously strutted on the stage to announce, "Miss Gus Bugler will now give you 'The Wind'". Just one member of the audience started to laugh, others quickly joined in. By the time I came on the stage to recite *The Night Wind* the audience could not stop laughing, especially as my first sentence was 'Have you ever heard the wind go woo-ooo – 'tis a pitiful sound to hear.'

Fig. 4   The original 'Hardy Players', circa 1914
Left to right, standing: Reggie Barrow; Mr. Prior (pianist); A. C. Cox; Monty Brown
Ladies left to right: Ivy Brown; Eileen Bugler; Gertrude Bugler; Dorothy Pauley; myself

Here is a copy of *The Parable of the Gypsies* – as far as it goes. It was hand-written on paper now yellow with age:

'And it came to pass a great war did break out, so that all the nations of the earth did go mad.

'So that in all the great cities and towns great numbers of soldiers did congregate.

'And behold the great city of Durnovaria did get her own share of them, and these same soldiers did cry out:

' "Wherefore is there naught to amuse us after we have worked hard all day preparing so that we may be ready to fight our enemies?"

'Thereupon one of the elders who did live in the South Street of that city took it upon himself to provide their amusement and he did annoy his friends saying: "Why do you not journey to the hut and sing and dance and make merry with the warriors?"

'And his cry did not fall on deaf ears for it came to pass that certain people did say to themselves ". . . are we not hot stuff? Therefore let us form a troupe which shall be called throughout the ages 'The Gypsies'"

'And so the troupe was formed (some of the members thereof being tall and some short of stature) to the great amusement of the crowned heads of Europe and the greybeards that did dwell in huts . . . till one day some of the tribe that did live near about did witness a performance of the said 'Gypsies' and greatly marvelled thereat saying ". . . cannot I and my friends do likewise. Lo! these 'Gypsies' do wax fat by the sense of their own importance", which did create jealousy in the land.

'And after many days this said tribe did arrange to give a great performance. But whereas they of the 'Gypsies' had been exceeding industrious and did strive day and night to improve, they of the neighbouring tribe did not work so and were unprepared.

'So they did come again to the 'Gypsies' and say ". . . come help us, for our own show is not ripe".

'Whereat the 'Gypsies' did grin up their sleeve, but for manner's sake they said we must be polite to them.

'Then they who did dwell under the Southern Cross and did journey many miles to help their kinsmen in their tribulation said ". . . wherefore oh 'Gypsies' do ye not visit us, for these Weymouth mummers make us tired!"

'And so it came to pass that the fame of the Gypsies did spread
to the four corners of the Earth, whereat the people of the towns did say
in the strange language of that country – "we don't think" '.

———————

There was little entertainment to be had in the 1914-1918 war. Concert parties were easy to transport to villages as well as to the soldiers. No scenery was required; a piano was always available as were all the well known songs of the time. Recitations were also on the programme, even a form of ballet dancing which I learnt at school.

I can still remember one recitation even now:

The Reciter

There was once a little boy whose name was Robert Reece;
On every Friday afternoon he had to speak a piece.
So many poems thus he learned that soon he had a store
of recitations in his head, and still kept learning more!
Now, this is what happened. He was called upon one week
And he totally forgot the piece he was about to speak.
His brain be cudgelled. Not a word remained within his head.
And so he spoke at random, and this is what he said:-

"My beautiful my beautiful that standeth proudly by
It was the schooner Hesperus the breaking waves dashed high.
Why is the forum crowded? What means this star in Rome?
Under a spreading chestnut tree there is no place like home.
When Freedom from her mountain heights cries
Twinkle little star. Shoot if you must.
This old grey head. King Henry of Navarre.
Roll on thou deep and dark blue crags of Drachonfell
My name is Norval. On the Grampian Heights.
Ring out wild bells! If you're waking
Call me early. To be or not to be.
The curfew shall not ring tonight.
Oh! Woodman spare that tree!
Charge Chester charge; on Stanley on.
And let who would be clever.
The boy stood on the burning deck . . .
But I go on for ever."

———————

Such was the enthusiasm of those days – and possibly to encourage a very little fair-haired girl – the audience would clap loud and long and shout 'encore'. This little poem was then given, which definitely caused much laughter:-

> *"Tu-whoo" said the owl; "tu-whoo" said his wife,*
> *"That rook down below leads a lonely life.*
> *A bachelor he'll live and a bachelor he'll die.*
> *Why doesn't he get married, we can't think why".*
> *So they cried to the rook with a loud "tu-whoo –*
> *Is there never a wife in the world for you?*
> *There's nothing like love if you'll only try.*
> *Why don't you get married – we can't think why".*
> *But 'eer the moon rose and the world was at rest,*
> *Mistress owl kicked her husband out of their nest.*
> *"Caw caw" said the rook, a sailing by.*
> *"Why didn't you keep single – I can't think why."*

––––––––––

'The Gypsies' provided entertainment right through the terrible war years. I remember I missed the excitement of appearing before audiences when at long last an armistice was to end the war for another twenty years or so.

Fig. 5   A studio portrait of myself in the early 1920s

Part Two: Peace Time

2.1 The Peace procession

In 1919 a carnival was held in Dorchester to celebrate peace. Many decorated cars made their way to be judged in the barracks square at 'top-o'-town'. We had a Ford car then which was stripped of its seating. Material was draped along the sides and back of the platform where the seats once were and flowers and foliage were added to make a riot of colour. My two sisters, a friend and myself were dressed in Grecian costumes denoting 'The Dawn of Peace'. The tableaux represented Justice, Wisdom, Goodwill and Light. As 'Light' I was seated by a hamper containing white pigeons which were released at intervals. This awarded us first prize which meant that we led the procession of cars around the streets of Dorchester and Fordington. When slowly passing near the trees towards Icen Way I was seen to shiver. The raindrops from the trees caused me to do so; unfortunately it was not a fine day. Such is rumour in a small country town – the next morning Saint Peter's church bell tolled for me!

Fig. 6   The 'Dawn of Peace' procession, Dorchester, 1919
Left to right: Eileen Bugler; Gertrude Bugler; Dorothy Pauley; myself

2.2 The original 'Tess'?

There is a saying that 'truth is stranger than fiction'. What could be stranger than that my mother, maiden name Augusta Way, lived at Bockhampton before marriage, helping her father who had a dairy near the lovely old Elizabethan manor adjacent to Kingston Maurward. In his youth Thomas Hardy often visited Kingston Maurward, passing by the dairy, thus seeing my beautiful dark-haired mother milking a cow. Tess was created in the mind of Thomas Hardy then. To Thomas Hardy it must have seemed to be a reincarnation of Tess when my mother's eldest daughter, Gertrude, played Tess in 1924 at the Corn Exchange, Dorchester. That could be why he became so fond of Gertrude.

All through these years I repeatedly heard references made by my parents to relatives I had never met, of a mysterious law suit, of a Kate, when my father would look at me and say, "How like Kate you are, poor Kate". Then he would become very sad, that sadness never to be explained . . .

2.3 Gertrude marries

In 1921 My elder sister Gertrude married her third cousin Ernest Bugler. Therefore she did not change her name when she was married at Stinsford church. I was her chief bride's maid. Eileen, my other sister, was also a bride's maid. We were driven in cars to the church, seemingly to me filled with people, to witness my sister's marriage vows. We were wearing turquoise-blue dresses. Very serious the words seemed to me; I had never read the marriage service. I knew I would miss my sister so much, the sister I loved. We were provided with hassocks to kneel on during the marriage service. Several times I thought it was over. Several times I stealthily put the hassock out of my way. I just missed falling over it eventually. The reception was held at the 'Central' of course. A lasting memory is of the bride's maids trying to cut slices of the wedding cake to hand around to the guests. The icing then was very difficult to cut with a knife as it was set very hard. The first few slices were very large!

It was found out later that Thomas Hardy would have liked to have been invited to the wedding. My sister did not think he would be interested.

2.4 Sister Eileen

At about this time my other sister Eileen had a 'miff' – as Hardy would have described it – with her boy friend and they parted. Gertrude invited her to come to Beaminster to attend a farmers' dance. She was introduced to a farmer who was a widower with a son of 18 years and a daughter still at school. Eileen accepted a very early proposal of marriage and the wedding was hastily arranged to take place at Stinsford church, a very quiet affair. I saw little of the church on this occasion. The car detailed to pick me up was made late by another guest; thus I arrived just in time to take a photograph of the 'happy couple' coming out of the church.

Stoke Abbott, quite near Beaminster, was a quiet picturesque little village nestling under one of the highest hills in Dorset, Lewisden Hill. This was where Eileen was to live, a few cottages scattered along the road, a church and a pub and that was Stoke Abbott. My new brother-in-law owned a large horse because he was a large man. He rode around the farm on it overseeing the management of it by his son. At times her husband was troubled by gout; and then my sister had to learn nursing as well. I remember he quite scared me at first, being a very tall thick-set man with a rather gruff voice. As I lived in a town I wore high-heeled shoes. He would look down at them to tell me they were of no use for walking in the countryside. "If you come to the countryside you should wear country shoes." he said.

One day my sister Eileen, knowing that I loved horses, suggested I had a ride on her husband's horse, which was a very docile animal. After encountering some difficulty even mounting the animal I found I had little control, my short legs seemed to be of little use and the ground below seemed a long way down should I fall off. But I would not tell my sister how very apprehensive I was feeling. The horse ambled down the village, past the church, then turned the corner to stop in front of the village pub – and was prepared to stay some time seemingly. I managed to persuade the animal to move sooner than was expected, to return to the farm house. I learned quite a lot about my brother-in-law's habits that day and was I glad to get off his horse. My legs ached for quite a long time after that.

2.5 More school

It was in 1921 that the arrangement was made for me to complete my schooling at the Beaminster Grammar School, where the Oxford Senior Examination would be held in 1922. So I stayed with my much-loved sister Gertrude, not to be entirely parted from her as I had feared. She now lived in Riverside Cottage, a very old small building overlooking the River Brit, which flows through part of Beaminster, on its way to the sea at West Bay. The Grammar School was situated quite a way from Riverside Cottage, almost at the other end of the town. It proved to be very different from the private school I had left in Dorchester. The boys and girls studying for the Oxford Senior seemed very interested in me because I arrived halfway through a term which they could not understand as it was so unusual to them. I was not used to seeing teachers walking around in caps and gowns. Nor was I used to walking to various classrooms. When it was raining getting to these separate classrooms could be quite an adventure.

The head master was very much in evidence. He would preside over assembly at 9 am, when a hymn and a prayer was the order of the beginning of a new day. We all wore school uniforms and discipline was very strict. The French master would allow no English to be spoken in his class. One Monday morning he decided to talk to me, in French of course. He asked me whether I had attended

Fig. 7   Beaminster Grammar School, 1920s

church the day before. Not understanding a word I very shyly said in French "yes". Then he continued the subject by asking "why did I go to church – to pray?" I answered "No". The class and master were now having an unusually hilarious time listening to my misplaced answers. Eventually the teacher asked "did you go to see other ladies' clothes?" to which I replied "Yes". My 'audience', some of the pupils that is, told me afterwards what I had said and how funny it was to them. I cannot say that it was all that funny to me. There is a vast difference in being able to speak a language and understanding it.

My school days were now nearing their end. We pupils at Beaminster Grammar School received our examination papers for the Oxford Senior Examination and were segregated in one classroom with a teacher, no speaking, just writing and handing the papers to him when finished. Then the long wait for the results during which time I returned to Dorchester. When at last the longed-for letter arrived I learned that I had passed the exam – distinctions in History and French I think it was. Quite a few failed although their mathematics was way ahead of mine, but their French was the trouble. Our teacher could speak French fluently but he could not teach. Some teachers are like that, so I've heard.

2.6 Family life; learning to drive

I convinced myself that I would never get married. My poor sister Gertrude was very ill during the nine months of her pregnancy, which I witnessed all the time I was at school at Beaminster. My mother arranged for Gertrude to be brought to the 'Central' for the birth of her first grandchild. A nurse was engaged for the confinement. Eventually, after many long days, a second doctor was asked to attend. He immediately administered drugs to put her out of pain and the baby was eventually born. Although they knew the child was not normal they tried to make her live. Fortunately she died at birth.

The year I left my school days behind me (1922) was a year of much adjustment. My father often drove my mother and me to Beaminster and Stoke Abbott on a Sunday to be with 'family'. I believe the car was a Humber, a very heavy four-seater car. It had real leather seats, a hood which could be moved over the passengers if it rained and a running board along the sides of the car which enabled passengers to get in. The road to Beaminster, and it has not changed much over the years, is still quite hazardous in places being very winding through the villages of Frampton and Maiden Newton; then up a steep hill to travel for miles over Toller Down which can be very dangerous in the winter. Impenetrable fogs

Fig. 8 Myself (left) and sister Gertrude in a Carley 2-seater, circa 1932. It is thought that the car was made at a garage in High East Street, Dorchester.

can arise. Then a sharp turn into the road to Beaminster, nestling under the hills of Dorset. It wasn't going down the hill into Beaminster I dreaded, it was coming up out of the town. Hook Hill is a very long hill slowly getting very steep at the top where there is a sharp bend. To drive up this hill the car had to have its lowest gear engaged. My father found great difficulty in engaging this gear and was inclined to rely on the brakes. The last time this happened I looked down the hill to see another car coming towards us. Father had the foot brake under control but he seemed to forget the hand brake. Thus we were gathering speed backwards. After what seemed to be an eternity he at last remembered he had a hand brake, and to turn the car towards the hedge where at long last we came to a stop. I had never experienced such fear and I refused to get in the car when driven by my father.

For this reason my mother decided that I should learn to drive. She arranged with our next-door neighbour – Tilley the motor engineers – for one of their best drivers to teach me. I was given five lessons on driving a car forward, one on reversing, and I was on the road. No driving test in those days. I remember driving on the straight stretch of road leading to Warmwell Cross from Weymouth at 31 miles per hour. My instructor told me I was driving too fast! He explained that anyone can drive a car fast but a good driver knew how to drive a car slowly and he wanted me to be a good driver – well perhaps? Anyway, I drove until I was about 93 years of age, had a few near misses, but never an accident. But I still feel fear when I am driven up Hook Hill.

At first my father did not take kindly to my driving the car. He kept upsetting my concentration by telling me how to drive. Usually my mother eventually had to intervene.

I do have quite vivid recollections of my father's idea of driving a car. Some of them are worth relating. When crossroads loomed into sight he would put his foot on the accelerator to get over the junction as fast as he could. To negotiate a corner he would drive on the wrong side of the road apparently to see what was coming around the corner. On any steep hill he would invariably miss his gear, the result being a journey backwards down the hill temporarily out of control. For a long time I barely exceeded 30 mph. Eventually I found I could drive at 60 mph – if I had to. The roads in the early 1920s were as they had been for many years, almost country lanes, definitely not as they are today – so changed in parts of Dorset.

2.7 The Hardy Players and London

In 1923 Thomas Hardy presented 'The Hardy Players' with his one-act play *The Famous Tragedy of the Queen of Cornwall*. This play was too difficult for amateur players. I think even professional actors would also find it to be so. There were three female ghosts on one side of the stage trying to chant in unison and three males on the other side likewise. The words were more than difficult to hear. I was given a small part, that of the Damsel who came on the scene to deliver a message.

I believe it was known that one of the Hardy Players would make trouble whenever she could. As a very jealous and little liked lady she made me, a sensitive and very shy teenager, very unhappy until several of the Players told me she delighted in making trouble. "Take no notice of her" I was told. I felt happier after knowing this. This play, [the '*Queen of Cornwall*'] as others had been in the past, was performed in London as well as Dorchester and at Gertrude's suggestion I accompanied her, my very first visit to London.

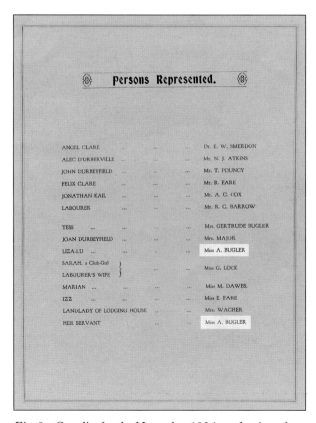

Fig. 9   Cast list for the November 1924 production of "Tess" in Dorchester

We went by train – it seemed a long journey to me and a very exciting one – to be one of the Hardy Players. At the end of the performance I was approached backstage by a charming lady, very smartly dressed in black; she seemed to know it was my first visit to London. "Where do you want to go?" she asked. "The Tower of London and Westminster Abbey – I love history" I answered. She talked about the play a little, then wondered why my sister, Gertrude Bugler was not in it. I said "Because she is married now and is going to have a baby." That was what she really wanted to know. Another Hardy Player, Mr. Barrow, asked me how I got on with the lady I was talking to. I said "I thought she was very nice, very interesting". Then he said with a twinkle in his eye "She was a reporter." I was very upset. I thought in those days reporters were always men. The next day her interview with me was recorded in the Daily Express.

The next year, 1924, was to be one of the years so very vivid in my memory. Thomas Hardy presented his own dramatization of *Tess of the D'Urbervilles* to the Hardy Players. He insisted that my sister Gertrude should play Tess, although she was no longer living in Dorchester. The rest of the cast he chose himself. This dramatization was performed only by the Hardy Players. I witnessed (in 2001) a performance of '*Tess*' which was supposed to be the one we did, but it definitely was not. I did not like it at all. I was cast as Liza-Lu, the sister of Tess. Thus we were sisters in life and sisters on the stage. As the understudy for Tess I read the part many many times at rehearsal, when my sister was in Beaminster. One Player remarked that our voices were so alike, if he shut his eyes he could think it was my sister saying the words.

Two very exciting events happened before '*Tess*' was staged in Dorchester. Dr. Smerdon, who played Angel Clare, arranged for a visit to be made by some of the Hardy Players to Wool Manor (now Woolbridge Manor), then a farmhouse. The wife of the farmer was obviously far from welcoming. She probably believed, as many did at that time, that Hardy might include her in his future writings. Dr. Smerdon had never finished reading '*Tess*'. He read no further than Tess's little brother asking about the 'blighted star' upon which he unhappily lived. Yet he played Angel Clare very convincingly considering it was a very difficult character to portray. Maybe as a doctor he understood better than many could. The confession scene, in which Tess revealed to her horrified husband her unhappy past, was played in front of the 16th century fireplace in the very room where Hardy had imagined the scene when he wrote *Tess of the D'Urbervilles*. Thomas Hardy listened intently, obviously very deep in thought. After Tess's sobbing ceased there was a long silence. Never had she played this scene with more feeling than at Woolbridge Manor. I think she felt the atmosphere of the lovely old house causing her to give the best performance of that harrowing scene she had ever given. In 2001 I was taken to see all that is left of the D'Urberville mansion once again. Upstairs were the D'Urberville portraits of the evil looking ancestors of Tess, neglected over the years and hardly visible now. They are illustrated in the programme of '*Tess*' I still have. Now they are just a mass of paint. A pity they could not have been preserved in Dorchester Museum, but impossible because they are built into the wall.

The other exciting event was that Thomas Hardy requested that the entire cast should come to Max Gate, his home in Dorchester, to rehearse there. He was then a frail old man, not wanting to go to a dress rehearsal in the Corn Exchange where the Press would be present. So, one evening the Hardy Players were received at Max Gate by Mrs. Hardy. I took an instant dislike to her, for no reason then. The Hardys sat behind a table in the alcove near the large window, then covered by long curtains. The centre of the room was the stage with one exit by the door. We rehearsed, mainly word perfect, with the exception of one Player. He asked Thomas Hardy at the end of the rehearsal if he was playing the part as Hardy imagined it? The only reply Hardy gave was, "Mr Atkins, learn your part!". Personally, I thought his performance to be overacted, therefore unconvincing.

Thomas Hardy beckoned to me to come to the table. He asked for my script, saying, "I haven't given Liza-Lu much to say, have I?" He seemed to me, then so young, to be a very old man who sensed my acute shyness and love of acting. He added to the two words "Tess, Tess" which was all I had to say after rushing across the stage to throw myself in Tess's arms, the sentence "I'm so glad you have come home." Then he returned my script to me with a twinkle in his eye, saying "That's better isn't it?". I thanked him, feeling he, so shy himself, understood me, and was trying to help me.

To everyone's astonishment, Mr Dawes, our prompter, elected to take on himself to give a long rambling speech. He was on many committees in Dorchester, a rather pompous individual. He informed Thomas Hardy that he personally did not like the play at all. He continued that all the church people of Dorchester and villages around would not wish to see the play and that the book had already offended many.   He went on and on and at long last reiterated his first criticism, that the play would not be a success, to which Thomas Hardy quietly said "Don't you, Mr. Dawes?".

On Wednesday November 26th 1924 *Tess of the D'Urbervilles* was first performed by the Hardy Players at the Corn Exchange, Dorchester. I still have the programme. On the front page is just 'Tess' followed by the second page giving the programme:

> ' *Tess of the D'Urbervilles*', a tragedy in four acts with an
> after-scene by Thomas Hardy, O.M., being his adaptation for the stage
> by request, in 1894-5, of the Novel of that title, and hitherto unacted,
> which the Hardy Players have the Author's permission to produce at
> the Corn Exchange, Dorchester, on Wednesday, November 26th, 1924
> and the three following nights at 8 pm.. Doors open at 7.30 pm..
> Matinee Thursday, November 27th at 2.45 pm..'

There are several photographs included in the programme. The first is of a drawing by Sir Hubert von Herkomer RA of *Tess the Maiden*, depicting her standing in the doorway of the old cottage after the club walking, looking at her mother still at the wash tub. Then two photographs of Woolbridge Manor and two of the sinister looking D'Urberville women's faces on the wall. 'Tess' played to crowded houses; extra performances had to be given. Many prominent people came to see 'Tess' plus the London press, most of which praised my sister's performance as Tess. Later 'Tess' was performed at the Pavilion in Weymouth. The Hardy Players did not perform in London.

It was after one performance at the Corn Exchange I saw a not very

"THE FACES ON THE WALL."
(Chapter XXXIV.)

Fig. 10   The 'faces on the wall' at Woolbridge Manor, illustrated in the November 1924 'Tess' programme

tall man standing by himself side stage looking across the empty stage. His intensely blue eyes caused me to enquire who he was. 'Lawrence of Arabia' conveyed little to me then. Later, in 1935, I remember hoping against hope that he might recover after the terrible injuries he had received from his horrific accident. He loved speed, thus a very powerful motor bike was to end his life, the uncrowned 'King' of Arabia. At his funeral in Moreton village I saw the long procession walking behind the coffin to the graveside. Winston Churchill I recognised, looking very grim and sad. I wonder if, even then, Churchill could have foreseen the coming war and knew he had lost someone who could have given untold help.

2.8 The Jealousy of Florence Hardy

It was just after 'Tess' was staged in Dorchester that negotiations were in progress regarding my sister Gertrude, playing Tess in London with a professional cast in a series of matinees. Florence Hardy by this time had become insanely jealous of my sister. Apparently she imagined Thomas Hardy was becoming infatuated with her. Perhaps Florence could not understand that the Tess he had created in his mind gave him so much pleasure to be able to see after all those years since he had created her. Florence was actually driven to Beaminster, unknown to her husband, to beg my sister not to go to London as Tess. All sorts of excuses were made, except the truth, and eventually my poor sister agreed to write the letter of refusal. Thomas Hardy must have thought her to be very ungrateful. He died not knowing the truth. Many letters have revealed, after Hardy's death, that Florence Hardy was a neurotic woman. Her insane jealousy of my sister was all in her mind. Gertrude saw Hardy as a genius, as did all the Hardy Players, certainly not the image Florence created in her unhinged mind. Had Gertrude gone on the stage at this time I feel certain she would have become a very successful actress. She had a wonderful gift which was destroyed by an insanely jealous woman. A dream was also destroyed for me. I too loved acting. I missed the Hardy plays terribly. Life went on without very much to look forward to. 1928 was the year Thomas Hardy died. My sister was with me and the Hardy Players at the funeral at Stinsford Church. In those days black was the only depressing colour to be seen at funerals.

In 1929 Florence Hardy's conscience must have pricked her very much indeed, for she arranged that my sister should play Tess in London but with another producer who got in touch with my sister to suggest she played Tess at the Duke of York's Theatre. This time she did go to London and was very successful, billed as Hardy's Tess. It was to be my second visit to London, to stay with my sister for a weekend. She did not like touring afterwards and eventually returned to her home at Beaminster.

I had heard '*Tess*' so often, so had no desire to see it again, but the 'talkies', as the films were then called, could only be seen in London. No-one was available to accompany me to the Tivoli Theatre where *Bull Dog Drummond* was being shown, so I went by myself. There were circular supports to the building partly obscuring the screen on which I saw elongated faces at times and heard distorted voices. A few years ago I saw that film again on television. What a lot of overacting and what silly plot it was – and in black and white of course. Coming out of the Tivoli I was to face London at night. I had been told not to speak to anyone, only a policeman. Why, I had no idea! I walked and walked, seemed much longer than in daylight, but no policeman could I see. I was beginning to feel frightened and that I might have taken the wrong direction. At long last I beheld the burly form of a very tall policeman. I asked him if I was in the right direction for the Duke of York's Theatre? "Over there, my dear, only the lights have gone out" was his comforting reply.

Fig. 11   Gertrude Bugler, a London stage photograph, 1929

2.9 More memories of Dorchester

I shall describe the Dorchester of the early twentieth century, as it was before I left, and which I remember so well. There were more private houses then in South Street and Trinity Street. The business premises were occupied by families living in rooms above their shops, and the Town Council was run by Dorchester people. It was a very prosperous market town. Sunday – no shops open – a day of quietness apart from the church bells of St. Peters and Fordington ringing out their message before eleven am. Then the silence of Sunday. Nobody walking down the streets, no vehicles down the roads, only birdsong from the surrounding trees where once the Roman walls stood. It was a silence difficult to understand or even imagine now.

Many were in church or chapel, while others were cooking their Sunday roast, something looked forward to all the week. It was a special treat, either roast lamb, pork or beef, with uncontaminated vegetables, and puddings or tarts to follow. Every Sunday I went to the Congregational Chapel, now the United Church in South Street, with my grandfather. The sermons were long, about three quarters of an hour. The seats became harder and harder; those sins I had to listen to, which I could not understand – to a child it was very bewildering. One of my cousins, who lived in Southampton, came on holiday to Dorchester. He too had to go to chapel with grandfather. When there was a long pause in the sermon a loud crunch was heard breaking the silence. My father's garden in Trinity Street grew apples, some of which had been given to his nephew by my father before my cousin very reluctantly went to chapel. Eating an apple in chapel was hardly expected in those days, but boys would be boys even then!

At a festival in the Chapel the children were assembled nearer the pulpit. Each had a leaflet on which the hymns they were to sing were printed. A number of children sitting for some time created enough rustling of paper to distract the preacher. So in despair he leaned over the pulpit and said "Children, look at your leaflet". They did; then he continued "Do you all remember what you have read? Now sit on it." He gained the silence he desired.

My father had a large garden running parallel with the Bowling Alley Walks. In it were greenhouses growing grapes and, of all things, a pig sty where father kept his much loved pigs – in the middle of Dorchester. A Roman coin was dug up in this garden.

Wednesday was a very busy day in the commercial world – market day. This market was held on the west side of the Weymouth Road, quite near the beginning of South Street and near the Junction Hotel, which still stands today. It was a truly noisy scene. Cocks crowing, pigs grunting and squealing, calves bellowing, sheep bleating, farm workers yelling the Dorset dialect, auctioneers' raucous voices hoping to be heard above all this din to sell their various pens allocated to the said sheep, pigs and calves, and the loud protests from the horses being tied up to have a much deserved meal from their nose bags.

It was the meeting place too for the farmers, who rarely left their farms except to go to market. They too added to the din, shouting to each other. One thing they could be certain about – they would get home safely even if too drunk to drive. Horses are very intelligent, they know the way home. In the market house, a large building, were boxes and boxes of butter made on the farms carefully rolled in half pound weights, cases of eggs, all genuinely free range, bags of potatoes, swedes, turnips, anything the farms could grow. I have memories of seeing cows driven along the South Walks road to the market, their udders so full of milk which could no longer be retained – a cruel practice this. No milking till they were sold, then they were milked in the market. There was a cattle market on Saturdays and Poundbury Sheep Fair, all bringing prosperity to Dorchester. In later years horses and wagons decreased, giving way to the modern world of today and the motor car.

The Dorset dialect was rampant in the market, much of which could not be understood today. "Git on and bide still" was often heard of a carter trying to control his horses. "I be Darzet an' I be proper proud o' it"; we Hardy Players spoke the Dorset dialect too, the only time it has ever been spoken on the stage.

Fig. 12   The Bugler shop, South Street, Dorchester, circa 1910. Unknown person.

37

Part Three: Country Life and Another War

3.1 From Dorchester to the Country

In the early 1930s my mother became suddenly very ill. I saw her carried down the staircase on a stretcher to be rushed to the County Hospital in Trinity Street. A boy of seventeen years had the same complaint, peritonitis; he died but my mother survived.

My mother's health deteriorated causing my parents to retire from the business which was carried on by my brother. This was the worst decision ever taken. Eventually it resulted in the destruction of the lovely stone building known as The Central Hotel. I had no desire to work with my brother so I decided to go with my parents in 1931 to 'Weyauwega', a house at Crossways, which was totally unlike the Crossways of today. Then it had a shop, a garage, a row of houses and bungalows called Dick o' the Banks, plus one or two bungalows in line with Weyauwega and a farm. Weyauwega means 'here we rest' in the Maori language. Actually, we didn't rest for long.

I had a feeling I would like to train as a nurse, but had never seen anyone dead, the thought of which rather frightened me. My mother often would say, "Dead folk won't hurt you, it's the live ones who do."

Poultry was kept on some spare land adjacent to Weyauwega. I became interested and sent to the North of England for a few Ancona hens costing five shillings each plus a cockerel at ten shillings thinking a Reverend Wilson could be trusted to sell good stock. The County Poultry Instructor on examining them told me they were useless and advised me to buy where I could see and examine the stock to be bought. White Wyandottes from a near neighbour began my future poultry career.

The years 1933 and 1934 had very hot long summers. Weyauwega had a very deep well which ran dry in both of those years. There was a sheep dip about two miles away towards Warmwell village. Our Austin 12 was stripped of its back seats. Water containers were standing everywhere, even seven pound one-time jam tins were balanced on the running boards. Then I drove the car and my father to the sheep dip at about 8 am. We filled the containers with water which was used to drink, wash, clean, and for the toilet, plus the poultry. I have never been able to waste water since.

A poultry farm with seventeen acres of land, about half a mile from Owermoigne, came up for sale. The late owner died of cancer at thirty years of age. When I saw him I remember seeing him place a match box under all that was left of his arm to be able to light a cigarette. My father bought this farm which contained four very large poultry houses. Attached were two very big wired runs to each house. One run could be 'rested' at intervals when required. An incubator room and rearing house was nearer the house plus some appliances for rearing chickens out of doors. The first week at Sunnybrook Poultry Farm was strange indeed. No post – we had forgotten to notify the Post Office, no electricity, no telephone, water difficulties regarding the pump which supplied the house, only an oil lamp for night use and not even the house complete. The light Lister engine and generator was quickly installed from Weyauwega to give light and gradually order was very slowly made. There were gorse bushes, silver birch and brambles everywhere, even to the front door. Young oak saplings too. All had to be cut down to make the winding drive which now exists. So Weyauwega was rented to an army officer at Bovington Camp and we went to Sunnybrook, in Moreton Road.

I ventured down to the village of Owermoigne when there was a New Year celebration in the village hall. There I met the village school teacher who taught the small number of pupils who all walked, some several miles, to school in those days, in all weathers. "Careful what you say to anyone in this village, they are all related to each other", she warned me. And it was so because no one moved out of the village for the men folk were employed on the surrounding farms receiving very low wages. Thus cousins married cousins year after year. There were some truly Dorset characters in the village then. Walt was one. A true countryman with a wealth of knowledge regarding the countryside unknown to books.

One hot summer day my father decided to burn up some rubbish which, caught by a varying wind, burnt a large area. The gorse bushes caught alight, a terrifying sight, and the fire gained ground rapidly. Walt then took charge, lecturing my father about starting fires in summer time when the ground was so dry. We were trying to beat the fire out with various spades and rakes with little success. Walt shouted out, "We'll 'ave to git Darchester vire brigade out; we kant put it out no hows." Suddenly the wind changed direction, blew back over the charred ground and thus put out the fire. We could hardly believe it. Our black and red faces were a sight to behold let alone the rest of our anatomies most uncomfortably overheated. On another occasion Walt came up the lane to hear voices where he least expected. I was weeding the gravel path accompanied by a wireless set to relieve the monotony of the job and the loneliness. Says Walt, "I cum away up 'ere to git away from two wireless zets I recken. Me neighbours never stops yappin' all day an night, each zide o' I". He was living in the middle thatched cottage approaching Owermoigne. Evidently he did not appreciate the company of his talkative neighbours. All this talk would be in the true Dorset dialect, reputed to be the nearest to the Saxon tongue.

On one side of Walt's 'yappin' neighbours there lived a very old couple. The wife had her last child of many at fifty years of age. They lived in the oldest cottage, sadly pulled down, where there was an inglenook hearth in which I sat to look up at the sky. Upstairs, a winding staircase and very small windows under the thatched roof. The winding staircase must have been a problem regarding a coffin. I used to cycle down to this cottage to get the daily paper, there being no delivery past the village of Owermoigne. On one occasion a horse was walking about the lane unattended. I spoke of this at the cottage, to which she replied in broad Dorset dialect "What 'ee zay? A hosse on the road. Now thick be proper dangerous. Must 'ave got out, wonder whose 'tis? Could upset the traffic." To my knowledge there was little traffic to be upset on the narrow country lane where cows were left to eat the grass along the verges before reaching their destination.

In 1938 I was persuaded by the County Poultry Instructor to enter six of my white Wyandotte hens in the Dorset Laying Trials which were held near Puddletown, covering a vast area of grassland. Hundreds of hens were entered of many breeds common in those days such as Rhode Island red, light Sussex, white Leghorn and many others. Each entry would be placed in a small wooden hen house containing perches and trap nests, giving access to small wired grass runs. Testing covered forty eight weeks. Attendants were allocated a number of pens each to record and observe conditions. The hen could help quite a lot. She would enter the nest and in doing so she would lift a shutter which descended after her, imprisoning her while she laid her egg. Loud and prolonged cackling brought the attendant who took the egg first, then let the layer free. My six were very tame when they came home. Every month a newssheet came from the Laying Trials making 1938 a very exciting year for me. My hens won a Gold Medal. There was no presentation as intended, just 2 guineas sent by post. Everything had to adjust to war conditions as rapidly as possible and a promising career in the poultry world was no longer to be.

3.2 War-time experiences and the poultry farm

As requested, in the afternoon of 2nd September [1939] I drove to the laying trials to collect my six hens. An eerie silence; no sound of cackling hens, a lost world of inactivity, silent, all seemed unreal to me. I felt deeply depressed. An unknown future menaced me, over which I had no control. Sunday 3rd September at 11 am; Chamberlain announced over the wireless that my country was at war against the might of Hitler's Germany. I had already become a member of the Womens Land Army in 1938, thinking poultry would not be kept in war conditions. This proved to be quite wrong. The few Accredited Breeding Stations set up by the County Council were eventually allocated extra rations of feeding stuffs to keep egg production going throughout the war.

As soon as the ARP [Air Raid Precautions] was formed in Owermoigne I joined and was made the one messenger to keep communications between Crossways and Owermoigne. Crossways then consisted of Dick o' the Banks Road and a few scattered houses. I was issued with the only tin hat available. It was very heavy. I never wore it. I kept it on the empty front seat of the car. I have a very vivid memory of seeing about six men of the village standing in a row with a hand gun – no rifle – passing it to each other after being instructed how to use it. So little was the country prepared for war. Many thought England would be bombed immediately. That was not so and for a while it seemed as if there was no war.

That was when, in 1940, a visit to a specialist was made when my mother's cancer was diagnosed. She was not told. After an operation she was given six months to live. After the first three months it was advised that she should be told. It was then that she begged me to end her life. I was in charge of countless morphine tablets and knew how many to give at 9 pm. every night. I told her I would but for the law, and I meant that. To see her suffering horrific pain till the morphine took effect was terrible. Animals are 'put down' in less pain, yet human animals are made to suffer a long slow death in agony. The District Nurse was my only adviser during this terrible time. She was wonderful, gave up her holiday until after mother's death. I shall never forget seeing my mother in her coffin. All the pain had gone from her face, she looked amazingly young and very beautiful. That is how I remember her.

During this agonizing six months I applied for a Womens Land Army girl to help on the farm. She was of little use; had evacuated herself from London to Bournemouth. She was not young and knew nothing of country life and was not adaptable. She came to work with gloves on her hands. I endured her for a fortnight. Bracken grew abundantly on the farm and had to be controlled by cutting it down by means of a hook. I showed my Land Girl how it was done, as close to the ground as possible. When I came out of the house after attending to my mother I found the tops of the bracken had been cut off, not the stems, which if left could harden quickly to make walking difficult. She asked "How do you tell the pullets from the cockerels when they hatch?" Being very fed up with her by then I replied "The cockerels crow and the pullets cheep" and she believed me till I just had to laugh. That decided me. She was creating more work, not less. I heard that she was posted to another farm where she was kept just one week. So I struggled on alone, with little sleep at night.

Another memory of the Land Army girl; she refused to enter one pen where there was a rather vicious white Wyandotte cockerel with his dozen or so hens. He would rush at anyone to use his spurs on any legs he saw. I told her to hold the bucket of food she was carrying near the ground in front of her, the cockerel would attack the bucket. But this she was too terrified to do and would not enter the pen. So I had to do the feeding myself. This cockerel I kept for several years for he threw excellent progeny. I called him Hitler.

After my mother's death, we heard that Weymouth and Portland had been bombed. My bereaved father expressed an idea that he would like to go there, and as petrol was not then very limited, I drove him in that direction. We were not allowed near. On the way home we called in to see my uncle, who lived in Crossways then, next to the garage. Suddenly an unearthly, frightening wail growing louder and louder pierced the quiet of that Sunday afternoon. It was the first time I was to hear the wail of a siren, a truly nerve wracking sound. My uncle shouted to us to go down the shelter, which was in the garden. I said, "I must lock the car first" which I did, then went down the steps of the shelter to feel the first thud of a bomb dropped not far from the shelter. Gradually the thuds of the bombs receded and there was a strange silence. I stood up from my chair saying, "Now we'd better sing *God Save the King*." Why I said this I shall never know, a strange kind of reaction to an uncanny, unreal experience.

I went to see if our late home Weyauwega was still intact. It was standing without doors or windows. A bomb crater in the nearby road was rapidly filling up with water from the mains water supply. Several people I knew came to me for help; they had lost their homes in the raid. I suggested they went to my home temporarily, adding "That is, if its still there". A retired admiral seemed to be helping too, so I drove my father home to find several people there already in a very shocked condition. Eventually, after cups of tea and a rest things were sorted out.

Dick o' the Banks Road [Crossways] was a sad sight indeed. The German bombs had destroyed the dwelling houses. That was the first time of many that Warmwell aerodrome was bombed. It was a day I shall never forget. The next day there was a 'phone call from Bovington to say the tenants of Weyauwega would be unable to continue to rent Weyauwega. The house remained derelict throughout the war.

On one occasion I was summoned to the ARP headquarters in Owermoigne. Seemingly there was no connection by telephone to the Crossways warden. I was detailed to make contact. I asked if I could drive with all lights available on the car. The headlights were fitted with war time light excluders. "Yes" was the answer. I drove down the lane as far as Owermoigne Church. There I was stopped by sentries. The village then had troops stationed there. They told me to put out my lights. Thus I drove up to Crossways, some two miles or so, without lights. Fortunately there was a moon above shining in the sky. I drove up to the garage where the son of the ARP warden was gazing up at the sky watching the searchlights. He said "What are you doing here?", obviously very surprised to see me. "Where's your father, Ken?" I asked. "Down there" he said pointing to the air raid shelter. By this time the warden was coming up the steps of the shelter. I delivered my message to which he replied "They should be ashamed of themselves

Fig. 13   Some of the Bugler family in 1940. Front row left to right: my sister Eileen with Christine Toms (my niece Diana's daughter); my father Arthur Henry Bugler; Ernest Bugler (Gertrude's husband/cousin and Diana's father), with Michael Toms, Diana's son; Geoffrey Bugler, a grandson of my father and son of another Arthur who could have taken the photograph. At the back left to right: Gertrude; myself; my niece Diana Toms; Philip Toms, Diana's husband.

sending a woman out alone on a night like this." By this time I'd lost my patience with him saying "If you had answered the 'phone instead of being in the shelter, I shouldn't have had to drive here". We had quite a wordy battle, then I turned the car round and drove home. Shortly after that the car skidded into a wall on one frosty morning resulting in a damaged back wheel. Many times was I stopped to be told by worried motorists that my back wheel was coming off. It never did. The Owermoigne ARP warden decided that as my car could only be driven at 30 mph in this condition it was no longer of use for ARP work. She suggested I should resign, adding "I feel, too, you have more than enough to do on your farm." How true. So I resigned.

My father accepted an undertaking which he had not quite understood. It involved delivering a Ministry form to every family in Owermoigne and to collect it when filled out, then to be taken in to Dorchester. It was not only the village but outlying collections of houses as well, such as those very near the Warmwell aerodrome and on the coast. This last collection of houses involved walking along the cliff paths, which I did instead of my father. Here I was to meet the brother of Winston Churchill. He ridiculed the whole procedure, saying, "If photographs were on each identity card it might make sense, this is just a waste of your time and of money". His brother, Winston Churchill was not then in power. To my dismay a somewhat elderly lady flatly refused to write down her age. How the authorities dealt with her I never knew.

RAF Warmwell contacted me to supply the officers' mess with eggs. I was promised left over bread etc. by way of inducement. Was I appalled at the waste – whole loaves were often included. The hens laid well on this diet; it helped enormously as far as feeding stuff was concerned. The Ministry of Agriculture took some time to turn over to war conditions.

At times petrol rationing caused me to catch a train from Moreton Station to Dorchester to see my relations there. On one occasion the train was at least an hour late. Many of the RAF personnel began to sing "Why are we waiting!" They ceased when the news came that Southampton [from where the train came] had been heavily bombed.

Inside the gate of Sunnybrook poultry farm there was a number of outhouses including a garage and a store for poultry food such as corn and dry mashes. This store had two or three wooden steps before the floor was reached, the object being to keep the food dry. One evening the floor of this store seemed to vibrate quite a lot which I had never known it to do before. "Was Bournemouth being bombed?" I wondered. Eventually we were to find out it was Southampton some fifty miles away. One of my 'Southampton' cousins was killed in that raid. He had driven to the Civic Centre. Later he was found dead, the engine of his car still running. He was known to have been carrying £50 which was stolen while he lay dead. For ten days no relatives knew of his death. He worked by day in the bake-house at St. Mary Street, Southampton. At night he drove to West End, several miles outside the City. No. 98 St. Mary Street was quite near a railway line. When sometimes on holiday there I would be fast asleep to be woken up by the rumbling and shaking of the old four-storey building by a near-by train rushing by. Yet this old building remained intact throughout the bombing of Southampton. A bank standing opposite across a quite narrow street was blown to pieces.

At this period the aerodrome was mercilessly bombed, as were the cities of my country. Night after night overhead was the drone of German bombers on their way to bomb their targets. During a late delivery of eggs to the aerodrome I saw the airman in charge of the kitchen gazing upwards with a shocked expression on his face. He said, "One a minute, poor devils who are going to get that lot!" After one raid all personnel were told to evacuate the aerodrome as fast as was possible. Delayed action bombs had been dropped. Quite a few found shelter in my home that night. They were all suffering from shock. There were no guns on the aerodrome with which to defend it then.

A summer night at dusk in 1945; the distant noise of many aircraft coming from inland roaring over the house, disappearing out to sea, all flying low and in formation. My father opened the side door, stood under the porch and beckoned me to join him. We watched this seemingly never-ending formation of aircraft pass over hour after hour. At about midnight my father decided he was too tired to stand watching any longer. It was then the nightingale started to sing from the trees in the little wood opposite the house. At intervals the frightened clucking of a pheasant joined in a combination of sounds I shall never forget, the wonderful songs of nature contrasting with the menace of war machines. The next morning it was announced on the wireless that the invasion of Normandy had begun.

Then the horrendous news came that two atomic bombs had been dropped on defenceless cities in Japan. It was terrible to think that such a cruel invention could destroy so much, cause so much suffering to helpless innocent people.

3.3 A Friend from Czechoslovakia

On one occasion, in the blackout, I heard a voice say "Can you tell me, where is the station?" I said curtly "You're on it" in as deep a voice as I could. I hoped he thought I was a man. I always wore breeches throughout the war. I was afraid he might be drunk. The time was 10.30 pm on Moreton station. Then he said "I do not mean this station, I mean the RAF station. I am a Czech and I do not know where I am. Can you help me?" I told him I was going that way to fetch my bicycle which I had left at a cottage near the station. We walked to the cottage during which time I learned he had escaped from Czechoslovakia. His name was Fransek Chmel.

When I unthinkingly asked him "How?" he said "I'm sorry I cannot tell you that." "I'm so sorry, I should not have asked you, should I?" "No" he said. "You should not!" That was one of the wartime restrictions which I was not used to then. He told me he spoke six languages fluently, finding English the most difficult. Then he asked how many I knew. I admitted I knew enough French to make myself understood, but not fluently. He seemed surprised. I suggested the reason to be that I lived on an island, not a continent where many languages could be heard. We reached the crossroads. I told him the aerodrome was straight on. He asked me if he might escort me to my home. I said I had a great deal of work to do when I arrived. I told him of the hundreds of eggs which had to be turned over by hand and of the wicks which had to be trimmed under the foster mothers in the rearing room. He said he would very much like to watch what I had to do so what could I do but say "Yes"!

It was at least a mile from the cross roads at Crossways to my home, so while pushing my bicycle down towards Owermoigne I told him about something I thought may be of interest to him – it was to me.

Farmers are rather insular; I certainly was. Farming was my only great interest at that time. I told him, at length, of my very worrying experience which had recently occurred. A very infectious disease of chickens had been detected in one pen of about a hundred young chicks. A sulphur-based compound should have cleared the trouble very quickly but it had not and the chicks continued to pass blood in their droppings causing their death.

This same trouble had been reported on another farm resulting in several vets and perhaps scientists, I never knew which, came to the farm. Fortunately I had kept strict accounts of everything that had happened and I was told that the 'Ministry' was very worried about these two outbreaks. I was given advice and eventually the trouble ended for me.

In those days, some sixty years ago, chick rearing was very different from the methods used today. No electricity on any of the farms then.

After I had put my bike safely in a shed near the farm gate Frank and I made our way to the 'incubation room' which was very well insulated and certainly warmer than the very cold night air outside. In this room were five one-hundred-egg incubators and a table. Out came a tray of eggs from one incubator onto the table and as fast as I could I turned each egg, the tray to be returned to the incubator as soon as possible to prevent cooling. Frank asked why I had to do this. "In nature" I replied "a mother hen turns each of her dozen or so eggs that are under her with her beak. I have to take the place of the hen." If the eggs were not moved the germ inside would die.

Then, with the aid of a torch, before opening the next incubator to repeat the turning of the eggs, I had to make sure that it was also showing the correct temperature, 103 degrees Fahrenheit. The paraffin heater and lamp at the side of each incubator also had to have a regular inspection. This completed we opened the door to the adjoining 'rearing room'. Here there were three-tiered wired pens, twelve in all. At one end of each pen stood a metal foster-mother. Attached to it were slit curtains of thick warm material allowing easy access to the warmth of the interior when required by the chicks.

The paraffin heater inside the 'foster-mother' needed great care – at least the flame did! If too much carbon formed the wick would lose heat causing the chicks to huddle together, even to cause them to die. Along the side of each pen were adjustable chicken troughs containing mash, available for the chicks to eat, as long as it was daylight. As a change sometimes grain was scattered. Constant access to water was important. When weather permitted, a trap door could be opened to allow the older chicks to sun themselves in a wire cage outside the brooder house.

I nearly forgot that Frank was there. He was so quiet, I being so busy seeing that all was well. He asked if he might come the next evening. I again said all of everything he had seen would be repeated for it was the busiest time of the year on a poultry farm. He came. He told me with great bitterness that our Prime Minister, Neville Chamberlain, had utterly betrayed the Czechs. He told me there was the equivalent to the Maginot Line in his country, that the Czechs were fully mobilized to resist Hitler's invasion and that the Czechs would have won the war. At that time I could not believe this for English people had not been told the truth. Fifty years later I knew he had spoken the truth then. He referred to Chamberlain as 'the man with the umbrella' with great contempt. For Winston Churchill he had the deepest of admiration.

After a long spell of silence he quietly said "Will you marry me?" "But we hardly know each other" I gasped. "You can't love me." "I do, very much" was his reply. I told him I liked him, would it not be better to know each other longer? Shall we write to each other? I gave him my address and suggested he came the next evening. I found myself looking forward very much to the next evening when he would be coming again. Hour after hour went by. I felt deeply depressed. He did not come. When I drove to the aerodrome with the egg order I overheard an airman say "The Czechs didn't stay long, did they!" Then I knew why he had not come. I looked forward to receiving a letter. No letter came. At Christmas came a Christmas card with an address. I wrote, still no reply. Lost letters were to change my life.

3.4 Bees and poultry

A swarm of bees on the branch of an oak tree began my bee keeping activities early during the war. A friendly nearby bee keeper took the swarm for me, brought a hive, ran the bees into it and there they stayed and increased over the years. Sugar was allocated to bee keepers during the war, honey being yet another precious food. Milk was no problem – straight from the cow by hand milking from the nearby dairy. We had to fetch it. Actually the rationing of food, felt so much in the cities, was almost non- existent on a farm.

The Rector of Owermoigne used to call to see my father. They both loved to talk about the countryside. I said I did not have much time to attend church services, in fact it seemed to me my bees always swarmed on Sundays. Such a lovely answer: "I feel you probably learn more from the bee's way of life than you would from my sermons."

Under war conditions the poultry farm was allocated feeding stuffs for 500 hens. The contents of the feeding stuffs grew more and more limited as the war dragged on. Fish meal, which aided laying potentialities, becoming almost non-existent. Old potatoes were not rationed so I bought these in ton lots to be stored in a shed. Potatoes grow shoots if kept over a period. These had to be taken off each potato, being poisonous to poultry, before being cooked in a large container. Actually they caused the hens to get very fat. I found I had to be very careful how much potato I added to the mash. Deliveries of pullets had to be made to the customers in the area, as well as sending some by mail. It was lucky that Moreton station was quite near. One customer wrote saying the pullets had arrived safely by rail (a hazard in those days) adding "they are such cheerful little chickens." I was tempted to call my farm the 'Cheerful Chicken

Fig. 14   Poultry at Sunnybrook farm, 1940s

Farm', but I didn't. When the extra hour of daylight became compulsory it meant that I could not go to bed till after midnight. The poultry had to be securely shut in every night. If not, a fox could cause the death of many. A fox kills for the lust of killing, not as most other animals do, for food.

A little gosling, of which I grew very fond, would follow me up the road to the dairy. When very young it would tire quickly and flop down on the road. I then picked it up and carried it till it recovered. Then it indicated it wanted to walk again, and thus we eventually reached the dairy. It must have been a comic sight, but there was no one to see it.

The house was very cold then. No central heating, a cold bedroom at night with a hot water bottle to warm the bed and an 'Esse' cooker which, being wrongly installed, caused endless trouble and little heat. The heavy black-out curtains too had to be in place every night.

The urgent ringing of the 'phone on one winter night brought me running downstairs. It was the ARP warden. "A bomb has dropped near you. Can you go outside and see if you can locate it?" I immediately put out the hall light, opened the front door to be confronted with the utter impenetrable darkness which only country dwellers know, accentuated by the wartime blackout. I returned to the 'phone saying "I can see nothing at all." The next day it became known that the bomb had killed a farmer at Warmwell, some two miles away.

The war slowly dragged on over the years. Hitler's invasion of Russia brought some relief to our British cities and aerodrome. Warmwell aerodrome was eventually taken over by the American Air Force. Over the years the wooden army huts were erected nearer and nearer to the farm, so near in fact that I remarked that the hen houses, which were quite large, could be mistaken for part of the aerodrome. And they were! An enemy plane flew low and machine gunned them, one of the occasions when I hastily dropped to the ground.

Part Four: Peace Again

4.1 Meeting Frank Chmel again

And now at long last, and at the end of the war, I was in communication with Frank. He came to my home from an aerodrome on the East Coast. The journey, by rail, was a long one to Moreton station. It resulted in his not feeling very well. I became rather worried and asked him where I should contact if he became worse. He said "Warmwell RAF, but I will be better". Fortunately he was right. I remember playing on the piano on a Sunday afternoon to entertain him. I played various songs and a hymn which caused him to say, in a very angry voice "That is the German National Anthem." I stopped playing it immediately saying "It is a hymn here in England". His hatred of the Hitler regime was intense. He even went as far as to say "There would be no peace in the world while there are German people alive."

One Sunday afternoon he described the snow and beauty of his country and started to sing "I'm Thinking [sic] of a White Christmas", only he got into difficulties with pronouncing 'Christmas' and said it backwards so that it sounded like 'miscraft'. Anyway, it caused much laughter; and later when I had agreed to marry him he said "we'll have a little girl just like you, and a little boy". I was, to say the least, not expecting this because in those days such possibilities were not discussed before marriage, as they are in the present 'enlightened' times. Seemingly I must have forgotten that youthful vow never to get married. Time and circumstances change many things.

The next morning I asked him how he was feeling health-wise, to which he replied after very solemnly walking around the room seemingly to see how he felt? "I think that I do feel much better" he said. So I drove him to Moreton Station, little knowing that I was never to see him again.

I have often wondered what he had endured before he escaped to England – I shall never know. I wondered if he felt the same as he did in 1941 when we first knew each other. He did, and time had changed me. I had often thought of him over those years. He had told me I would love Prague: "It is a beautiful city". He had told me he was due to return to Czechoslovakia very soon and he did not know what he was going to find, nor what had happened to his country under the Hitler regime and now under Russian Communism. When he could he would return for me – meanwhile he would write. Those letters did reach me.

He returned to find his country short of food, short of everything. I sent him cigarettes which were non-existent there. He found his parents in a concentration camp. He could not recognise his father. Then I received a postcard,

Fig. 15　Fransek Chmel, 1940s.

a photograph of Prague on one side and a message on the other telling me not to write. At the very end of the card was the word 'later'. I never heard from him again.

There were times when a dream seemed so real I seemed to see him trying to tell me something which I could not understand. Many years later, on the European wireless programme I was to hear very late one night that those Czechs had perished under the Russian Communist Government then in power. The war ended in Europe, the Hitler regime was tried and punished. Hitler committed suicide, men returned to civil life over the years. I wish that I had not burnt his letters. They could now be part of history. I remember he wrote saying that he found writing in English to be very difficult, and that the room where he was writing was "full of noise" but that his thoughts were back in my England and "all around my house". I still have the photographs he sent me. Just before marrying Frank Woodhall, I destroyed the letters I had kept for so many years but I kept the colourful Christmas cards he had sent. Sadly, these were accidently burnt when mice were trying to inhabit the bedrooms upstairs.

4.2 Family problems

My sister, Eileen, had been called up in 1940. She was with the forces throughout the war. Now she had no home to return to. Her husband had died just before the war began and his farm was rented. She decided, after arranging everything with my father, to buy a caravan which would be sited very near my home. At that time there were but two bedrooms at Sunnybrook Farm.

Eileen was still making trouble for me whenever she could. I think she really enjoyed doing so. My brother had prospered during the war years, thus enabling him to buy another business in Dorchester – he rented the Central Hotel. My father insisted that Eileen should manage this new business and, to my great relief, she departed to Dorchester.

She then persuaded my father to give the Central Hotel site to one of my brother's sons – Geoffrey. Why she did this and why my father consented I shall never understand. Those were the days when the males of the family were given preference regarding inheriting property. I hate going to Dorchester to this day to view the ugly building which now stands on the site of the charming grey stone building which was once my home. My brother found her to be more than difficult and eventually sold the business.

It was my brother now who began to give me great anxiety. He had become an alcoholic. Often he would drive to Owermoigne when he should not be driving a car at all, in turn causing my father to face sleepless nights. I might add my father did not drink. It must have caused him deep distress to see his only son in such a condition. I asked for help from my doctor who told me he could approach Alcoholics Anonymous, but it could only be possible if consent was given by my brother. The years dragged on; the lies an alcoholic is so capable of telling continued. I found myself piecing information he gave against the truth. In fact I began to doubt others who were not alcoholics, a horrible state of mind to endure. The fear that he might kill innocent people when driving so dangerously drunk was very real. At last came a 'phone call to say he had suddenly died. The relief I felt cannot be described.

Our mother once said there was always trouble wherever Eileen happened to be. How true. She made my life utterly miserable, having all the time in the world to cause mischief, and she did. Nearing a nervous breakdown, I wrote to my cousin, Margery White, who now lived in Australia with her husband. They were Seventh Day Adventists and were willing to help me in Australia. My sister Gertrude, the sister I loved so much, came to me and pointed out that I contemplated helping the very thing that Eileen was scheming to do, which was to look after our father herself to get possession of the farm. I was longing to get right away from family. I felt I could not go on living under such a strain, unable to sleep at night and facing a long day of endless work. Then I thought again. Gertrude was right and I would follow her advice . . .

4.3 A holiday

In 1952 I arranged to go on a brief holiday instead of going to Australia. Now my father's attitude towards me very much changed. I had never travelled any distance by public transport in my life by myself. It proved to be a truly worrying time. After the long train journey to London, crossing London in a taxi and finally arriving at my destination, I was to find my luggage had gone astray. I found travelling exhausting. I had never been to sea. The near future looked truly ominous to me, especially after the life boat drill which was held before many had found their cabins. I had never seen such deep water before. Looking down from the deck was a new experience; water everywhere, but the sea was calm. Norway is so beautiful, the one country to which I could return. Hopefully the Norwegian fiords will always remain in all their beauty, never to be destroyed by Man's misguided love of destruction.

At Bergen we were entertained by some young Norwegian boys and girls, dressed in national costume. Norwegian folk songs were very well acted as well, being a delightful interlude. Some of our passengers indulged themselves well with Norwegian cream and later suffered the consequences. Britain was still on war rations in 1952. The fiords had such utter beauty, one of Nature's most exotic creations – unforgettable. The cascading waterfalls descending from such heights; the moonlight; it was fairyland.

Then to Copenhagen. Now I was not alone any more as another passenger, also single, had joined me. She had travelled more than I had and her help was much appreciated. Neither of us could speak the languages of the various countries we were briefly to see. This could be very worrying at times. Before we reached Lubeck in Germany we ran into stormy waters. My new friend, Helen, suggested we went up on deck rather than stay in a cabin. By this time the floor of the ship seemed to be coming towards me. The fresh air revived me. Many were sea sick, stewards in a minority and the dining room decidedly empty!

From Lubeck we went to Copenhagen and on to Amsterdam where we were due to leave at 3 am. for Southampton. We wandered along the canals admiring the city at night then remembered we had to return to the Central Hotel at a given time. We contacted a policeman. He could not understand English but hearing 'Central Hotel' directed us to a pub of that name. We again asked a clergyman who also directed us to the pub! Fortunately one man there understood English. We were hastily hustled into a taxi and thankfully reached the Central Hotel near the sea just in time.

Some of the passengers were decidedly merry at 3 am. At Southampton I was to contact a cousin living there. I never knew quite what happened; all I knew was that I was trapped in a lift by myself for what seemed to me to be a very long time indeed. The engineers told me not to worry. They would get me out before long. That 'long' seemed endless to me. To this day I avoid lifts whenever possible. Then home again, to the strain that had been lifted from me for a brief period.

4.4 Back to the farm and more bees

Over the years the one beehive had increased to ten. They were situated near the house under the hedge running parallel to the road. At intervals during the summer months the hives had to be inspected before the honey sections were removed after the heather season, and to have the honey extracted and bottled. On one of these occasions the dairyman's wife came walking down the road with her baby in a pram. I called to her that I had opened a hive. "Please don't come nearer" I cried. She did. A bee started buzzing around her head which she tried to drive away. The wrong thing to do, angering a bee. Fear made her perspire. Bees sting viciously if they scent the sweat of any animal. She was very frightened and called me to come to her. "Some bees will come with me if I do" I replied. She wasn't content until I went to her when I did my best to help. I think she must have had a headache afterwards. The baby was not stung as it wasn't perspiring like the mother. The next day, when my father went to the dairy for our milk, the dairyman became very offensive, every other word a swear word, to which father listened in silence. Then he quietly said "I don't understand French" and left the dairy. We heard nothing more after that.

It was during an August when a beekeeper came to see me. He had started to keep bees way back in 1900 and his knowledge was profound. I told him I had been reading endless books on bee-keeping finding them very difficult to understand. He suggested that those who wrote books invariable copied each others' theories on beekeeping; some could be misleading. Those who observed bees over many years did not write books. They acquired knowledge unknown to writers but no time to write about it. On one occasion when the cover of a hive was lifted a bee flew directly at my head. The poison was driven directly into my blood stream. I became very ill immediately and was violently sick. On reaching the Doctor's surgery four miles away the first question the Doctor asked was "Has she been sick?" This had saved my life. An injection was given and to my astonishment the doctor said "You must give up keeping bees. You will be allergic to bee stings for the rest of your life." My bee-keeping friend told me later that he had never seen anyone look so ill in so short a time. Reluctantly I found I had to give up learning any more of the wonders connected with the life of the honey bee.

Bees

I heard a strange noise, I went out to see
The bees were swarming on an oak tree.
Captured were they and put in a hive.
I thought to myself can they still be alive?

Beekeeper was I; I learnt more and more.
There were times when I did feel terribly sore.
A bee stings but once, then it dies.
That was when I opened the hive
One summer day
And I was lucky to be alive.

Only one sting but it poisoned me;
Quickly I was taken a doctor to see.
"Allergic to bee stings you'll always be" –
That is what he then said to me.

———————

If nature is abused her reaction is to destroy. I made the mistake of mating the highest recorded hens to very near relatives. Nature rebelled; 90% hatchability then death to the chicken. I then had to switch to another form of farming, egg production, eggs to sell 'free-range'.

4.5 Changes on the farm and another Frank

Now I had to change the poultry farm. From free range hens I turned to egg production. Customers came from miles around to purchase free range eggs. Among my many egg customers, one couple seemed very friendly. They came from Weymouth every week. The wife, having been a nurse, sensed I was very unhappy. She tried to encourage me to talk, but I was unable to. Then I noticed they no longer came for eggs. Some time went by then a letter came to my father. He tossed it aside saying he did not like letter writing. I read the letter. Suddenly I realised it was the husband of the couple who used to come for eggs every week. It was a heartbroken letter, saying his wife had died of cancer. The writer probably thought father would understand. I told my father he should answer this kind of letter. Eventually I replied. The next weekend Frank Woodhall came to see us. He seemed to be a very lonely, unhappy man. My father liked him. After the death of his wife he went to live in Salisbury having been moved there by the firm he was working for. He became very interested in poultry farming and usually turned up every weekend. I was glad of his help too. He in turn interested me in photography, at which he excelled.

At long last electricity from the grid became available. Frank suggested I drove down to his bungalow near Weymouth to view the various fires and cookers available, about which I knew nothing then. Our Lister engine only gave us light. I nearly missed meeting him. I was waiting at the wrong turning, but somehow he thought that might happen. I felt very relieved when I saw him coming from the entrance of another road. He was very helpful in so many ways.

When he asked me to marry him he waited till nighttime. It was 29th February. Leap Year in those days was considered the year when the woman could ask the man to marry her, so just a minute after midnight he asked me to marry him. He said afterwards that he was wondering if I would be doing the proposing. I took quite a time to say "yes".

Leap year

Over the years they come to me,
Ghosts of the past so vividly.
They smile and wave, and are gone again.
Why did I not say? Was I to Blame?
If I had said yes where would I be?
Far, far away in a wronged country.
I would not have lived, neither would he.
But that is past now, it is just history.

The years had passed when he came to me.
So sad and lonely and shy was he.
A long time to me he was just a friend
Yet over the years that had to end.
Long last I said yea and I wondered why.
He smiled and then said with a sigh
"'Tis past twelve o'clock, another day
And you did not ask me, I did say!"

———————

My sisters decided that they would look after my father who was now becoming frail with age. Permission was given to build a bungalow for farming purposes. It was built quite near Sunnybrook. Frank felt quite upset after a visit to his lawyer. "You are building a bungalow on land which is not yours, therefore the bungalow could be claimed by your future wife if disputes were to arise." Then Frank said, "But he has never met you, has he?" and cheered up considerably after telling me. He evidently had made up his mind that I would not be capable of doing what the suspicious lawyer suggested. We laughed about this, but it was the Law after all. We married at Weymouth Registry Office in 1962, quickly over a quiet wedding, just my two sisters there. That was what I wanted. It proved to be the happiest twenty-five years of my life.

4.6 Destructive mice

Just before my marriage to Frank Woodhall in 1962 I decided to burn the many letters I had received from Czechoslovakia some 20 years earlier. I have deeply regretted doing this for those letters could be history now. And later, mice were responsible for the burning of the colourful Christmas cards sent to me during the war years. In the bedrooms of Sunnybrook there are chests of drawers built into the outside walls as well as open spaces with doors giving access from the bedrooms. Various discarded objects such as unfinished oil paintings were stored behind the bedroom walls as well as the writing case containing the Christmas cards from Frank Chmel along with a lot of rubbish enchanting to mice. They took possession and built their nests. They were discovered when the house was being painted. Then the mouse traps were kept busy. One of my helpers descended the staircase holding a trap in each hand gleefully shouting to me "I've got five!" There are some hazards connected with living in the countryside, mice are the worst – or perhaps rats. Bats can take possession, and they did. I watched them leave the roof space at dusk flying away never to return – so far. Dormice too have tried to creep indoors, to be firmly sent away.

It was decided that everything which had been contaminated by the mice must be burned. A bonfire also consumed the little writing case containing the four Christmas cards and a post-card of Prague from Frank Chmel. Fortunately a photograph of him was mounted in a frame which I can still look at, and also an

Fig. 16   Myself and my husband Frank Woodhall, 1980s

oil painting given to me, so life-like, of my husband Frank painted by my friend from Brixham, Frank Pullen. It is hanging in my dining room. It was exhibited in the Torbay area and it shows my husband in a pub with an empty glass in one hand and a cigarette in the other. Frank Woodhall did not drink or smoke.

Of late I have noticed, on television especially, that any reference to the betrayal of the Czech nation seems to be ignored entirely should anything connected with this period in history be broadcast. Chamberlain, like so many previous politicians, seemed to know little of the 'far country' he spoke of at that time, yet he betrayed it to the infamous Hitler, not allowing the Czech people to fight for their own freedom. As Frank Chmel told me the Czechoslovakian army and air force were mobilized and would have won the war against Hitler. Instead Hitler annexed the Czech armaments as well, taken to invade Poland, the Low Countries and France. A year of infamous 'peace' followed with little done preparing for the war to come. Then the man whose warnings regarding Hitler had been ignored came to govern the country – Churchill, the man so admired by Frank Chmel. Why England was not invaded remains a miracle, attributed undoubtedly to the 'Few', those wonderful Royal Air Force men.

4.7 Snow

It was on Boxing Day 1962 that the countryside became white with driven snow. The serene silence which only nature can summon to her aid descended on the countryside, the landscape glittering white day after day. The deep drifts of snow blocked the narrow country roads. Only tractors could penetrate some of the distances. We were just about settled in our bungalow only to find, despite all new regulations regarding water installation, the inlet to the bungalow was to be solidly frozen for the next two months. Yet Sunnybrook suffered no shortage of water. A hose pipe had to be attached to the kitchen tap, through the open window to give water to the farm as well as to the bungalow. The farm fast became a nightmare. Egg production ceased. All poultry had to remain locked in their houses for safety regarding hungry foxes. Two buckets of heavy water balanced the carrier, who had to take them to the hen houses time after time. Usually it took us the whole morning. Then the food was taken, to keep the hens eating all day, otherwise cannibalism could easily arise. The delivery of poultry food became more than hazardous as time went on. At one point there was just a hundredweight left. Thankfully a delivery was made just in time.

When fetching our milk from the dairy I took a walking stick hopefully to prevent me sliding on the icy road. The farmer's little girl said "If you fall down with that lot there's plenty more." There was – a huge tank full of milk, no collection by lorry being possible. Anyone from the village could have free milk if they were able to fetch it. Many did. The rest of the milk had to be thrown down the drains.

Yet during that freezing cold weather, no-one had even a cold. Maybe the bacteria causing such was also frozen. Many wild birds died. I remember seeing a thrush trying to eat the frozen top greens on a Brussel sprout plant which just appeared above the snow in our vegetable garden. Other birds were trying to eat acorns which had fallen to the ground, which they could see but could not reach through the ice.

When the thaw came it was at night. A tap had been left dripping in the bathroom. Just by sheer luck, not being able to sleep, I happened to go into the bathroom just as the water was about to overflow from the bath onto the floor. The water pipes underground now sent out cascades of water all around the farm. Just another hazard of the many attached to the joys of farming under arctic conditions.

My father became very frail after that very hard winter. He was taken to Cerne Abbas, to a nursing home, where he eventually died in his sleep. The cost of that nursing home, where he was well looked after, was £12 per week. Almost unbelievable today. An electrical fault was the reason it was burnt down before my father's clothes could be collected.

4.8 The end of the farm

Now another hazard, a viral disease. There was no cure for fowl paralysis. I watched the hens when at point of lay suddenly fall paralysed unable to get up and eventually die. No disinfectant could clean the heavily infected land. It could no longer be used for poultry farming. The farm was sold and we returned to Sunnybrook to live.

Now Frank and I were free to lead our own lives but we did not get the neighbour I had hoped for. He should have been a naturalist, a very nice man. Instead we got an estate agent, or to use a modern expression 'a neighbour from hell'!

He so angered me over the years that I avoided him entirely. Before the farm had been sold there had been an application for a building estate, which I certainly had no wish for. Fortunately this had been refused. Yet this estate agent got permission to build the house that he wanted. I had to endure the resulting turmoil of building for many months.

Because I would have no contact with him whatsoever a letter arrived from him regarding boundaries. "Aren't you going to answer it?" asked my husband. "No" I replied. "That is what he would like me to do. Then he could make trouble for me". Another neighbour did answer his arrogant demands and was very sorry that he did so.

Several years passed by during which Frank and I often took coach holidays with members of the National Trust, to tour England, Scotland and Wales, and to get away from an unwanted neighbour. The roads then were not as crowded as they are now. The historic houses that we were taken to see were not so commercialised as they are today. In fact we had our holidays when travelling was comparatively safe and very relaxing, holidays to be remembered.

Frank slept happily during the neighbour problems but I endured many restless nights over which I had no control.

We returned from one of the holidays to find we had a new neighbour, very different from that estate agent we had endured for many years. Now I was able to sleep at night.

On returning from another holiday we found an open trench across our front drive. Gas had arrived and with it central heating all over the house. Running a home became a joy compared to the conditions that we had endured in the past.

Part Five: Illness and recovery

5.1 Cancer

When under stress of any kind I noticed I had pain and swelling in my stomach. This continued for some years, gradually increasing. A hysterectomy in the old County Hospital, Dorchester, revealed the presence of cancer. At Poole Hospital an operation to insert radium was unsuccessful. For that operation I was taken to a very large room containing many patients but they were all fast asleep. I was the only one awake. Apparently a decision had been taken that as I was in no way apprehensive, a pre-med would not be necessary. I asked the nurse "You will put me right out, won't you?" After that I remembered nothing till I became conscious again. Then I was told I must have day treatment at Poole Hospital. So quick was treatment then, I had hardly returned home from Poole Hospital before the 'phone call came telling me the time for treatment the next morning. During that August of 1979 I was taken to Poole for treatment by many drivers down country lanes to avoid the tourist traffic. Each visit to the hospital increased much discomfort till I told the nurses I could no longer control myself. This was reported to the surgeon in charge, the answer being "She must have the full treatment." I was given tablets and instructed on no account to take more than three, then I came home. I became very ill and my doctor sat down in my bedroom saying "I must read up about the tablets". He took quite a time doing so, then said "You must take another tablet".

I said "But I was told at the hospital that I was not to take four!" To which he replied "You must take it." I did. That doctor, I am sure, saved my life.

My husband was wonderful during my long, slow recovery from cancer. He would drive to Dorchester to buy anything I fancied, to tempt me to eat again. I was six stone in weight. At

Fig. 17 Myself dressed as a scarecrow collecting for charity at an Owermoigne Street Fayre

long last I was able to walk a little further every day. I literally walked myself back to health. After five years I was medically free of cancer. Poole Hospital was then appealing to the public to donate money for a much needed scanner. A colossal sum was needed. I felt I must help in some way. I drove to various nearby villages making door to door collections for the Poole scanner. So many asked me to tell them of my recovery from cancer. They too had relatives suffering from it, from which it was rare to live in those days. I sent well over £1000 to Poole Hospital.

Then I became very worried indeed. I was told it was against the law of the land to make a collection of money unless associated with some society for that purpose. At that time a police van came to Owermoigne every Thursday afternoon. Knowing this, I decided I would go to the Police and tell them I did not know the law about such matters. I approached a very tall burly policeman who looked down at me, and said, with a twinkle in his eyes "You look pretty honest, my dear, don't you worry, we'll do nothing about it."

Cancer

Many years gone by, was it 'seventy nine',
I knew my health was far from fine;
Cancer it was , to Poole hospital I went,
Day after day, a car was sent.
I knew not the road, so many there are,
The drivers, they knew, so much traffic to bar.

So thankful to be free of cancer was I,
I thought to help others, at least I could try.
Collect money for a scanner, that's what I dreamed
Which was not quite so easy as it all seemed.
Over a thousand pounds was given to me
Which I sent to Poole hospital, thankfully.

Then I was told I had broken the law.
I should not have collected that money at all.
A long time since the police car came –
On Thursdays it was, to stop in our lane.
I summed up my courage, he looked down on me
A burly policeman so pleasantly:
"You look pretty honest my dear" said he;
"You'll never hear about it, not from me"

———————

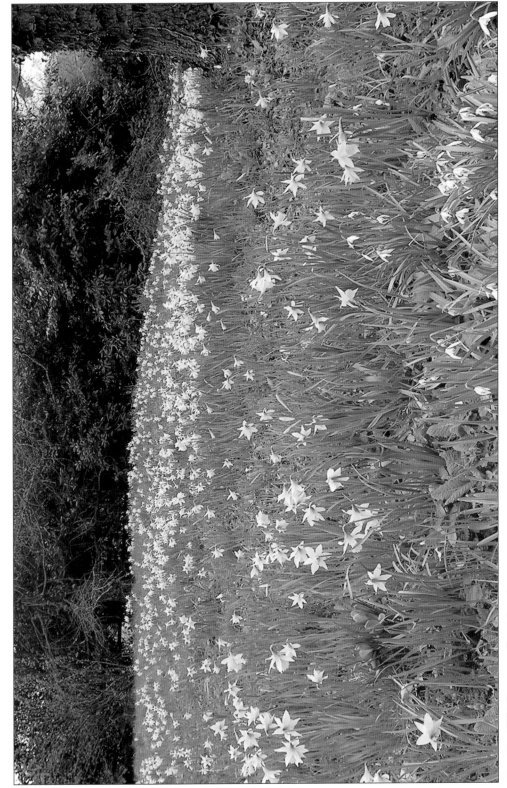

Fig 18   Wild flowers at Sunnybrook

Fig. 19   Early purple orchids at Sunnybrook

Fig. 20 My husband Frank Woodhall painted by Frank Pullen, 1970s

Fig. 21   A Purbeck scene, painted by myself, 1970s

Cancer had changed my whole outlook on life. I wanted to help others with cancer because I could speak from experience. A leaflet through the door decided me. A Dorchester doctor was petitioning for volunteers to help fight cancer with a course of lectures. Thus I became one of the early volunteers. The headquarters then was a caravan sited in Edward Road, Dorchester. For the friendly staff it proved to be very hot in the summer and freezingly cold in the winter.

There were street fairs every two years in Owermoigne. Over the years I wrote little books about Hardy and the countryside which were sold at the fairs in aid of Cancer Care. For about eight years I worked with the Cancer Nurse operating in Owermoigne, just staying for a while with those who had cancer, listening to confidences which would never be divulged, knowing cancer would prevail, and that a wonderful friendship would cease by death.

5.2 Painting and poetry

We had friends who spent a week with us and we spent a week with them over the years. Some lived in Brixham and some lived in the Cotswolds. Another Frank, Frank Pullen, lived at Brixham. He had been a member of the Birmingham Art Society, a very clever artist. He interested me in painting. I hardly knew where to start painting on the canvas when I began, but I had always loved drawing lessons at school. Each holiday there were painting lessons and much criticism, never praise. Frank's wife remarked that he never gave me a word of praise, which he should in her opinion. It was his way of teaching and it was the right way. My Frank would take photographs which helped subjects for my paintings. It was a very happy time for all of us, looking for subjects to paint in Dorset. Through Frank I entered yet another world, to be able to create a picture from nature. I enjoyed landscape painting; the unending colours produced by mixing paints, so many tones which could alter a painting in so many ways. I now saw nature in all its wonderful kaleidoscope of colours, the contrast of sunshine and shadow.

I entered another world when I began to paint. Light and shade, sunshine and shadow, and the world of wild flowers. Our garden became a wild flower garden. The many oak trees, some of which were each side of the drive, sheltered wild daffodils, primroses, bluebells, anemones, orchids and speedwell, to mention just a few. We opened our garden to the public in conjunction with the National Gardens Scheme. Two of my friends were at the garden gate taking the entry money and I was supposed to be showing the visitors around the garden. I had little chance to do this because one visitor monopolised my attention for most of the afternoon. After a quite learned conversation on his part he told me that I had a rare plant in the garden – a wild carrot. I said I did not know I had such a rare specimen and asked him to show it to me. We walked back to the drive and he pointed at his wild carrot. I said "That isn't a wild carrot, it's a pignut." I ended up digging him up a root to take away with him. Pignut grows in profusion here. It has a lovely little delicate white flower and an edible nut in the ground, probably ate by pigs hence its name.

You have already read some of my poems. Here is one I wrote about wild flowers:

Wild Flowers

So many call them weeds. To me they are wild flowers,
Brought to perfection by sunshine and showers.
The hedgerows are lovely throughout the year
Covered by wild flowers to me so dear.

The fields are now just one colour, green;
The farmers say never a wild flower must be seen.
But the verges, left uncut at long long last
Let the wild flowers at seasons their little seeds cast
For another year. So by seeds lightly blown
From seed may be years gone by are sown.
What a wonderful gardener Nature can be,
Grouping flowers and colours so beautifully.
Let them seed, let them seed and seed.
Never never call my wild flowers weeds.

It is bleak winter now; the wild flowers are sleeping
'Neath a green carpet of grass. They are keeping
Their seeds and beauty for another year.
Oh winter why so long so cold so drear?
The bare oak trees whisper, then scream to the gale –
My branches are breaking, oh be calm! Now all's well.
No all is not well, for no acorns do I see.
Will that in time mean the death of me?
My branches so twisted reach out to the sky
As they did years ago and I wonder why
Man must, with his horrible screaming saw
Sever such beauty with one terrible fall.

I gaze out of my window. The wild garden is gone.
A deep silence, soft snow falling, no bird song.
Little birds are dying, maybe some will live on
To sing when the winter, the long winter is gone.
I think of the summers of years long gone by.
Some thoughts make me sad, I nearly cry.
Memories of blue butterflies on the trefoil
Before Man spread his poison all over the soil.
Sand lizards and slow worms gently gliding by,
Glow worms glowing brightly 'neath June night sky.
Where are they all gone? Sadly no more to be seen
In my little wild garden when once more it is green.

Wild Birds

No nuts in the feeders, no birds are there
No woodpeckers little birds to scare.
April so cold, why did I not care?
It isn't so easy to try to get there.

The ground is uneven; I get my stick
Hoping to help me not fall over a brick.
I fill the feeder right up to the brim,
The birds soar above, they start to skim.

Down on the feeder they fly so fast
The nuts scarcely a day will last.
But it's lovely to see them back so soon.
All day they are there and then in the gloom,
They fly to the hedges to sleep at night,
My little feathered friends with colours so bright.

One unusual bird sighting was of great interest to us and we watched this over a period of about four days. Through the dining room window the bird table could be seen quite near. Not far away was a wooden gate giving access to the vegetable garden. On this gate perched a young cuckoo, the beak of which remained open most of the time to receive food from the poor little robin flying backwards and forwards to the bird table to drop food into the huge yellow beak which seemed to mesmerise the robin. A horse jumping nearby finally frightened the cuckoo which flew away. This episode happened in late summer when the cuckoo's parents had already left for a warmer country. Many times I have wondered how did that young cuckoo know where to fly by itself? Just one of the many wonders of nature.

5.3 Husband Frank

Frank Pullen was a portrait painter as well. He painted my Frank as a character in a pub. For exhibition purposes he labelled the painting 'Time Gentlemen Please'. Actually my Frank did not drink or smoke. A copy of this picture was made by Frank Pullen. He gave it to me and it hangs on the wall of my dining room. The painting of Frank is as he was before he became ill, as I shall always remember him.

When we drove to the Cotswolds to be with our friends we discovered many of the very remote villages, then unspoilt. Cameras recorded the honey coloured Cotswold stone cottages, so many pictures to paint. I felt I wanted to go home to my painting, yet I loved to be with my Cotswold friends. Those lovely friends are no longer here. There is one and she is in a nursing home. She does not know her own son when he goes to see her.

Frank always took over the household chores when I had the urge to paint. He would delight to tell me where I went wrong regarding perspective. We always had a friendly argument, ending because he proved to be right. We went to many art exhibitions. I actually sold some of my paintings. Those I liked still hang on the walls of Sunnybrook.

My husband's health had been deteriorating over the years. He became very deaf due to his war experiences, had recovered from heart attacks, and now one of his legs became very swollen, even to his thigh. One doctor seeing the many scars over Frank's body asked him to speak of his war experiences. Frank was reluctant to recall anything he had endured. He wished to forget. He did tell me he 'went over the top', that is he left his trench twice to try to get to the German trenches. Many were killed the first time. He was badly wounded the second time, waking up to find himself in a German hospital where the doctors were very kind. They healed his many wounds, after which he was a prisoner of war. Doctors and hospitals became very familiar to us. A middle-aged doctor told me he had never seen so swollen a leg as Frank's, yet Frank could still walk on it. My own doctor decided I must have respite, therefore Frank entered a nursing home for a week. I felt very lonely in the house by myself and I was glad to fetch him home. The next few days and nights he was very ill. Reluctantly I agreed to his entering the hospital, then in Princes Street, Dorchester. He lingered on for a very long time, heavily sedated. I drove in to Dorchester every day to be with him, latterly in a room by himself, but he did not know I was there. Once again, I was to witness cancer.

Over the years there have been occasions when I have resorted to express my feelings in poetry. The first was composed after I had lost my husband.

The Quiet Mind

Nature can take and she can heal;
Quietly she bides her time to seal
That loneliness which she knows so well,
Found so often in a lovely dell.

I went alone with Nature to be;
She gave me a quiet mind
Which so few see.
She says oh so slowly she
will heal and say –
"Tomorrow and tomorrow,
Another quiet day".

I look to tomorrow,
Shall I roam?
If I do, then I must be alone.
The loneliness of dark despair
Knowing, oh knowing he is not there.

I appeal to Nature, she comforts me.
Alone now, never, shall I ever be.
The years have gone by and now so I see
Wonderful Nature in her agony,
Of Nature, wonderful Nature in her agony.

Friendship

In the deep dark loneliness of utter despair
That was when I knew not where
To find relief, someone to care.
She came to me, she cared for me,
A true friend for the years to be
So long to find, and so dear to me.
In this strange world where now I live
There seems few who will even give
Time to listen – they all want to talk
Of their holidays, or if baby Willie can walk.
They rarely talk of the countryside.
Now that it's threatened far and wide
The birds of the air, will they soon be no more,
Only the cars and planes to roar?

5.4 Mental strain

The strain I had suffered and the loneliness of bereavement had me asking for help from my doctor. He, of the many people who gave advice, helped me the most. He would say to me "I want to see you on . . . [a given date]. Promise you will come to see me, promise?" Very reluctantly I would agree. He seemed to know I would keep that promise. On one occasion he asked me if I might commit suicide. My answer was "I haven't that courage". He insisted on seeing me time after time, medically making certain that I was able to sleep. Many people still have little understanding of a mental illness. That is why I am writing of it, having experienced one over a number of years. A deep slowly healing wound can be seen and treated over a long period. A mental wound is unseen, but it is just as deep, and it requires much longer to heal.

My sister Gertrude definitely did not understand I was ill. I still have the last letter she wrote to me on 2nd September 1991. She wrote:

> 'When you were here last and went <u>on</u> and <u>on</u> and <u>on</u> about my having called you a liar because I could not remember just one rehearsal out of many, many rehearsals. I was too astounded at what seemed to be the state of your mind to be anything but frightened, and could find no adequate reply at the time. For one thing what on earth does it matter whether I do or do not remember one particular happening of many, many years ago?'

On this occasion, my unhinged mind had returned to the rehearsal at Max Gate, requested by Thomas Hardy, in 1924. Gertrude could not remember anything about it, and told me I was lying. She almost convinced my father of this too. And she did not trouble to say she was sorry when another Hardy Player wrote of this rehearsal, thus proving I had not lied. This, as far as I can understand it now, caused me to hate my sister, the sister I had previously trusted and loved.

I found I could not drive to Beaminster again to see Gertrude, and I did not. Gertrude's daughter whodid understand that I was mentally ill suggested to me, in 1992 when Gertrude was nearing the end of her life, that I might regret afterwards not seeing her. Arrangements were made for Gertrude to be driven to Owermoigne and I was alone with her for a while. I believe she thought all was well between us again. Perhaps she forgot that I too could act – and that I was still in the grip of a mental illness. I have no recollection as to when my normal health returned to me, much of that illness is thankfully forgotten. Now I am told I have a wonderful memory and health too.

5.5 Counselling

For several years I attended a Community Centre at Acland Road in Dorchester. This centre helped elderly people to gather together, probably promoting friendships for those living alone. An ambulance would call at a given time, picking up members from the surrounding countryside as well as in Dorchester, all to arrive at Acland Road to be welcomed by a trained staff of carers for a day. A mid-day meal, always very wholesome, and various courses were available, such as exercises for those able to take part, discussion groups, painting – anything which might encourage older folk to join in.

I met some very courageous people who knew that the remainder of their life was to be confined to an invalid chair, the result of a stroke or worse. Others with dementia, happy in their own little world; a world not shared by the relative probably caring for them. One I well remember. She must have been quite beautiful when young. She truly enjoyed her meals which had to be restricted for medical reasons. She would smile at many but seemed unable to converse with anyone. When in the ambulance all of a sudden she would loudly clap her hands, the rest of us nearly jumping out of our skins, if that is the correct explanation. I saw her suddenly very quickly disappear into Dorchester when she should have got in the ambulance. Eventually she was found, but did not come back to the countryside by ambulance. She lived alone in very remote circumstances. When she began wandering miles across the countryside she had to be taken into care where such disabilities were treated by trained staff.

Another meeting was with a very intelligent lady. She was unable to walk, under no delusion as to her future. At present there is no cure for multiple sclerosis. She told me she came with her husband to Dorset because they admired the books and

Fig. 22 Myself painting at Sunnybrook, 1980s.
The painting was sold.

poetry of Thomas Hardy, adding "He was a horrid man wasn't he?" I was able to enlighten her regarding the untruths she had been told. Quite an interest became centred around Hardy by the time I decided to leave.

Another, a truly wonderful lady, was totally blind. I often would talk to – or rather listen to her. Once I asked her "Which is it the worst to be, blind or deaf?" Surprisingly to me she answered "They are both as bad as each other my dear." Frankly I do not agree for I am partially deaf; some voices I can hear, usually deep voices. If I go to lectures, and I have had to go to some Hardy lectures since I was made an Honorary member, I have sat still for some two hours or more unable to hear a single word spoken by the lecturer. Did time drag. How I wished myself elsewhere, more than anything possibly writing some letters which should have been written long before. To return to that courageous blind lady; blindness means total dependence on the kindness of people. This courageous lady lived alone, a widow dependent on carers who would dress her in the morning, come again to cook her mid-day meal and lastly, to prepare her and help her into bed. Otherwise she would be by herself. I watched her using her knife and fork to pick up the food she could not see. It was a revelation to me and I knew then, as one who deplores deafness, that it is preferable to being blind. I can see the wonderful pictures nature paints in the countryside, I can see to read books, I can see to turn off the television when it is definitely not to my liking and only too often it isn't.

Acland Road

And soon I shall be ninety five.
Yes, I think so, I'm still alive!
I see so many, far younger than I
Who rarely complain, not even sigh.
I look at them wondering 'why oh why'?
There is no answer, no one ever knows
Why Nature cares not, deals out such blows.

The blind lady wants to talk I see.
I tell her I'm deaf: which is the worse to be?
"They're as bad as each other" she answered me.
Others there are with strokes to bear
Confined for life to be in a chair.
Yet they come together just to be where
They find people so kind, those who care.

———

5.6 The family quarrel

Here I find I must return to Dorchester for a while, just my after schooldays. An unknown aunt, Aunt Melina, came into my life. She belonged to those relatives who were not to be known. Actually, I did not like her, so unlike the other three aunts – rather uncouth I thought.

Now that I could drive I had to drive my father anywhere he wanted to go. Aunt Melina and her husband now farmed at Dewlish. Father was invited there to indulge in his pet hobby, shooting rabbits. On one occasion he was invited, with others, to stand in a circle in the middle of a hay field where the last of the grass was standing, in which cowered quite a lot of rabbits and hares. These were driven out by dogs to be shot while trying to escape. Father, heedless that men could be in range of his gun as well as the rabbits, disobeyed all rules regarding shooting. Aunt Melina shouted to me to stop him shooting. I told her he would not listen to me; she would have to stop him. He was never invited to 'shoot' again.

Gradually my aunts and uncles became just memories over the years and the 'family quarrel' was not to be revealed by them, but by granddaughters in 1986. Aunt Melina married late in life, according to those days, at 32 years of age. She had two sons. George Voss, one of her sons, married and five daughters were born. Two of these daughters elected to drive to Beaminster to 'claim kin', as Hardy might have recorded it, with my sister Gertrude who was very much in the news regarding her connections with Thomas Hardy. Eventually they came to see me. It was arranged that we should meet at Kingcombe which was to be sold. I drove my husband through Dorchester down to the Yeovil road, passing through the villages of Grimstone, Frampton and Maiden Newton, up a very steep chalk hill, turning left at the top to descend to the little sleepy village of Toller Porcorum where a right handed narrow lane eventually took us to Kingcombe. My thoughts turned to my mother. Often I had heard her say, "When we went to Kingcombe . . ." Now I was to see Kingcombe without knowing anything about any connection.

We were quite glad to get out of the car after driving through such narrow twisting lanes, glad indeed we had not encountered any farm machinery. It would have been disastrous there being no room for two vehicles to pass each other. The first building which attracted my notice was a farmhouse, a barn and farm buildings standing in a field. It was the first photograph I took on that lovely day in May. I had a strange feeling about this farmhouse which would not leave me. It was as if I belonged. My two cousins joined us and we all walked slowly around Kingcombe. It was sad to see these acres without animals, buildings neglected, old milk churns rusting away, uneaten hay stored in a dilapidated barn, such hay not seen today for it had been made of meadow grasses now so rare. The late farmer had died at

92 years of age leaving the land free of contamination by modern farming methods. I remember seeing on the ends of two barns stone human heads set high in the stone wall and I wondered why they were there. We went inside the 'Long House' dated 1400. It too was in a sad state. Such farm houses are rare indeed. Mansions of that date remain but rarely farm houses. Upstairs there were large holes in the wooden floors, so much perished by age and neglect. Downstairs in the kitchen there was an inglenook hearth above which, attached to the ceiling, was a bacon rack. The floor had flagstones, the ceiling had dark oak beams across it, the windows revealed the thickness of the walls. The farmland was rich with wild flowers and wild life, deer in the woodlands, many species of wild animals, birds such as sparrow hawks and buzzards – none had been disturbed.

At that time the Press had covered Kingcombe's unique value so well that donations of money were gladly given to help preserve some of this farmland. So Kingcombe Reserve was formed for all to enjoy in the future. Sale boards were numerous, the hamlet having been divided into 'lots'. Prices soared at the sale.

My cousins had, over the years, been assembling a 'family tree'. Information had been gleaned from the tombstones in Toller Porcorum churchyard, also in various places in Dorchester. A will proved that Thomas Way farmed at Toller in 1904 and his father before him, possibly in the late 1800s. A copy of this will was given to me. Here it is, the will of Thomas Way of Toller Porcorum in the County of Dorset, part of which reads as follows:-

> "I give and bequeath all my real and personal estate of whatsoever consistency and wheresoever situate to my dear wife Ann Hayward Way for and during her life, and from and after her demise I give unto my son Frederick Thomas Way a legacy of £100 and subject thereto I find my executors named to pay and divide the net proceeds of my said estate unto and equally between my four daughters Susan Ann Eliza Greenwood, Melina Olga Voss, Annie Hayward Brown and Augusta Lydia Florence Bugler, in equal shares but subject nevertheless to the conditions that out of the share of the said Melina Olga Voss my executors shall pay to my niece Ada Wallbridge the sum of £50 and I appoint Arthur Henry Bugler, of South Street, Dorchester, in the said county of Dorset, Confectioner, and George Henry Harding Greenwood of the town and county of Southampton, Grocer and Baker, to be executors of this my will, and I revoke all former wills by me at any time heretofore made and declare this only to be my last Will and Testament."

At the beginning of that century £100 was a great deal of money and this will caused a bitter quarrel in the family, one brother and sister having no communication with their three sisters for many years. Father sometimes would recall the time when he went to London. Aunt Melina had taken the dispute over the will to the High Court in London. She lost because father produced a letter which, when read by the Judge caused him to comment "Mrs Voss has made mountains out of molehills". That will, first seen at Kingcombe, revealed to me something my father had never told me, that he was one of the executors.

5.7 Kate

Not very long before my sister died in 1992 two people drove to Beaminster to see her. They told her they were trying to assemble a family tree, but could not find anything about Kate Bugler. Gertrude had the same surname. Newspapers often wrote articles about her connection with Thomas Hardy, causing them to hope there might be a relationship. Gertrude told them the little she knew, which enabled them to continue their search. Evidently certain certificates were shown to her, for she remarked to her daughter Diana afterwards, "Well, at least they were married, I always thought they weren't".

On 19th August 1992 I was present at the service of Thanksgiving for my sister, Gertrude. As I walked up to this lovely old church in Beaminster I noticed some flowers had been placed on the steps. They had come from Hardy's Cottage at Bockhampton, and his Dorchester home, Max Gate.

A very strange thing happened to me recently. I was put in contact, by my cousin Margery, with a childhood friend of hers who used to live in Dorchester. A rather frail lady came, from the Cotswolds, to stay with me for a few days. She had made a scrap album of newspaper cuttings relating to the Hardy plays that were performed in Dorchester in 1923 and 1924. A cutting of the then Prince of Wales with Thomas Hardy and, something I did not know even existed, a photograph of myself wearing long dark plaited hair over my shoulders, taken when the *Queen of Cornwall* was produced in Dorchester in 1923.

My niece Diana often drives from Beaminster to Owermoigne to spend time with me. On one occasion she brought with her a large cylindrical object saying "I found this while sorting out a drawer and thought you might be interested. It means nothing to me!" After Diana had gone home I examined the strange object. To my surprise several photographs and documents fell out. The first photograph I examined was of a young couple. The young woman was

Fig. 23   Ernest and Kate Stevens, 1890s

wearing a 'boater' hat kept on by a hat pin, a veil drawn over her face, a high necked blouse and leg o'mutton sleeves. Her right arm was resting on a book, her left clasping an umbrella, gloves on her hands and a skirt reaching to the ground, quite full at the back, probably a bustle. The young man was wearing a cap and had a Victorian moustache. He was sitting on a chair with his legs crossed showing he wore boots. His right arm was clasping a walking stick, his left carefully posed behind his right leg. Both look somewhat strained possibly because they had to maintain a set facial expression for a considerable time. Photography in those days could be quite an ordeal. Another photograph was of a small child. She was dressed in Edwardian clothes. She looked strange around her eyes, not a normal child I thought. She seemed to have been photographed in front of a conservatory because there are plants in pots behind her, enclosed by glass panels. Yet another photograph revealed a marriage and death certificate. The marriage certificate was of Kate Adelia Bugler and Ernest William Stevens. The death certificate was of Kate Adelia Bugler. Then I knew. I was looking at a photograph of my Aunt Kate – the Kate my father would never talk about except to say "How like Kate you are; poor Kate.." He would seem to return to a past which I would never be allowed to share.

The next time Diana came to Owermoigne I enlightened her regarding her unexpected 'find' when she elected to sort out a drawer. "Was there any way of contacting these two strangers?" I asked. She thought she might have their telephone number. If so, she would ring them when she returned to Beaminster. This she did. They were very pleased she had made contact with them. Eventually, this resulted in Peter and Petrina Stevens coming to see me in my home in Owermoigne. Peter was trying to find out more about his grandfather's first wife, Kate. He had no idea where she was buried. He knew his grandfather, Ernest, loved Kate very much but that was all. I told him I knew my grandfather and grandmother must have been buried in the Dorchester Cemetery situated on the east side of the Weymouth Avenue just outside Dorchester. I added "I imagine Kate might be buried there too, but I don't really know." Peter finally sent me the results of the research he had carried out into his grandfather's affairs. Henry Bugler (my grandfather), the youngest of six sons was a very kind, understanding man who had the misfortune of marrying a very difficult lady (a grandmother I do not remember). Grandfather was a staunch Congregationalist and a Deacon at the then Congregational Church in Dorchester, now the United Church in South Street. They had three children, Arthur, Henry and Kate. Their mother was not young when she married, maybe that might account for her behavior regarding her poor unloved daughter.

Kate was born in 1873 at 1 Princes Street, Dorchester, then a confectionery business with living accommodation above the premises. Ernest was born in 1874 being the son of James and Ann Stevens of Downton in Wiltshire. Ernest's father was a paper maker. In about 1894 Ernest was apprenticed to a men's outfitter shop in Dorchester. This was Genge, still standing in Dorchester, a large premises with entrances in High West Street and Princes Street. The word 'Genge' is still to be seen above one entrance. Kate lived just across the road on the corner of Princes Street, helping in the shop, as well as other duties, with her father, mother and two brothers. Did Ernest go into the shop to buy some of the delicious confectionary of those days? I have a strong feeling that was how he met and fell deeply in love with Kate. Their meetings remained unknown to Kate's parents, mainly because Kate probably sensed that her mother would not 'approve' of a mere draper's assistant as a future son-in-law, which is what she would judge him to be. Her judgement quite wrong as on many other occasions.

So the lovers kept their love a secret. It must be remembered that little was revealed to the young people of those days regarding sex, as it is today. Two young innocents, deeply in love with each other. The inevitable results, Kate finding herself pregnant. Terrified and frightened she knew she would be blamed by her mother. They always blamed the woman in such cases. Life was cruel in those far off days. When her plight could no longer be hidden, grandmother's wrath descended on the poor innocent girl, whose total innocence had been her undoing.

Hastily, a wedding was arranged at the Congregational Chapel, just witnesses – no guests for certain from Dorchester. They were married on 24th September 1895 when Kate was 23 years of age and Ernest 22. For some strange reason Ernest's address at the time of the marriage was Oatlands, Weybridge. Did grandmother then take charge of Kate? I feel she did. Grandmother was a domineering, stubborn woman. It became known to me that she was responsible when grandfather lost a great deal of money. He was negotiating the sale of a house he liked for their retirement years. Grandmother continually found fault, delaying the sale for a considerable time during which the private bank holding some of grandfather's retirement money, failed. They then had to retire to a much smaller home, 3 Cedar Park Villas, now no longer in existence, which I remember as a child.

Kate's condition was not to be known by the people of Dorchester, reasoned my grandmother. It would be bad for trade and worse for her husband's position in the Congregational Chapel. Conceal her by day. At night, when dark, she might be allowed to go out. Continually being scolded for her so called deceit, the poor girl would have to endure the religious side – that she was a sinner. That the facts of life had never been revealed to her would be ignored by grandmother. That was not spoken about in those times.

Kate was taken to Park Villas, Melcombe Regis, to give birth to her baby. There she died on 21st December 1895. The cause of death was peritonitis and nephritis as a result of the birth. Her death and disgrace must never be known in Dorchester, and it was so. Her coffin was brought to Came Halt, just before Dorchester Station was reached, then transferred by road to Dorchester Cemetery, again before Dorchester could witness any strange happenings – and on Christmas Day, the one day no-one was likely to be in the cemetery. The population of Dorchester on Christmas Day would either be in church or chapel, otherwise at home attending to the Christmas Dinner; definitely not in a cemetery.

Kate was hastily buried in an unmarked pauper's grave, Plot 306. Her husband, now living in Wiltshire, was not informed of her hasty secret burial, otherwise why should he buy a double grave space for £6-12s-0d [£6.60p] on January 4th 1896? With the thought that he would be buried later with Kate? Three days later this plot was sold to a Mr. Trevett. Grandmother by this time must have told Ernest that he had a baby daughter named Hilda, that he was to take her to Downton where he was staying with his parents. On no account would grandmother bring up the child. That was the duty of the father's side of the family. And it was so. It was obvious that little Hilda was mentally as well as physically retarded. The stress on Ernest must have been colossal, only 22 with a little backward child to care for over the coming years. He asked for help from a doctor, who advised him to marry a strong minded woman who would look after him and the child. Within a year or so he met and married Annie Elizabeth Barham from Brading in the Isle of Wight. She was 5 years older than Ernest, and definitely had a very strong personality. She decided she was not going to be responsible for Ernest's retarded child by another woman. Her unmarried sister, Edith Sara Stevens, was selected to care for the poor little retarded unwanted Hilda Stevens. Hilda died when she was 21 years of age, on 8th December 1917. Edith lived on till 1926, as did Ernest. They were all buried in the same grave, in the churchyard at Downton Baptist Church.

Peter and Petrina Stevens, who had done so much research on Kate's life and death, decided they would visit Dorchester Cemetery where they hoped to locate Kate's unknown grave. They wanted to make arrangements regarding a memorial stone. Imagine their surprise when they found a tombstone already there. Seemingly it had been there for a very long time too. I have a strong feeling that my grandfather knew about this. Grandmother Bugler died several years before my grandfather, enabling him to enjoy some happy years doing exactly as he wished. He loved his only daughter and did not wish her to be forgotten.

As if to prove my theory, in April 1999 Diana had again elected to sort out another drawer. She found a State and Division Account of Henry Bugler deceased. Unfolding it she saw the name of Stevens and began wondering if this was in any way connected, so she brought it to me. The connection was without doubt there. My grandfather had left the same amount of money to his two daughters-in-law as to Edith Stevens who was caring for Hilda Stevens, the retarded child of Kate and Ernest.

Peter and Petrina came to see me again. They were going to visit Kate's grave and wondered if I would like to come too. Quite honestly, I do not like graveyards at all. My mother did and would often of a Sunday take me to Dorchester Cemetery where she would talk of those she remembered. I had little interest, mainly because I did not know them. As Peter and Petrina had driven a long way, I did not like to say no. We stood by her grave side in silence, all of us probably thinking of poor Kate's unhappy life. A man's voice penetrated my sombre thoughts. "Do you know where [name not remembered] grave is? I can't find it anywhere". I looked at him, not liking his abrupt interruption of my reverie and said "No, I don't", thinking that was the end of the matter. It did not prove to be for he was one of those individuals who never stops talking. He went on and on about the relative's grave, the lifetime of the one buried there and finally, of all people, Thomas Hardy. I listened to his truly silly untrue judgement of Thomas Hardy. I was told he knew someone who worked at Max Gate. She should know what a mean, horrible old man he was. When at last I was able to get a word in edgeways I told him what I thought of the untruths he was uttering. I told him the Hardy Players knew the real Thomas Hardy more than any other, that I knew that to be true as I was the only one alive. I added he was a very shy clever man. My two friends said afterwards they had had a very interesting time listening to this somewhat unusual discussion.

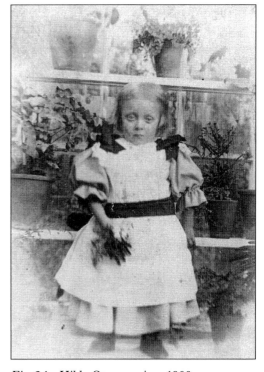

Fig. 24 Hilda Stevens, circa 1900

5.8 A bit of local history

Recovering from this somewhat bizarre encounter, I asked Peter and Petrina if they had ever visited Maiden Castle. They had never heard of it. I suggested it might interest them as it was older than Stonehenge and it was quite near the cemetery. I rested in the car while they walked to view Maiden Castle. They were gone a long, long time and they had managed to find something they thought belonged to the inmates of long ago. Both thought Maiden Castle to be of far more interest than Stonehenge. Then I suggested they might like to see Maumbury Rings which was also quite near. Apparently they had driven past it countless times but did not know it had been a Roman amphitheatre and was far older than that.

I remember seeing deep blue information boards which were erected on the approaches to Dorchester. In their place now are larger posters with just trees on them which convey nothing of any interest. Since the 1960s far more of Roman Dorchester has been uncovered and the unique Town House near the Council Buildings has been terribly neglected over the years. Hardly a signpost to guide those interested to it. When will the people and Town Councillors of Dorchester understand that Dorchester is absolutely unique. No other town in the world has so much to offer tourism.

My Dorchester

Oh Dorchester, my Casterbridge, what future now?
The day is gone when it was the plough.
I look deep into the future, what do I see
For my Dorset may be hope and prosperity.
Tourists from all lands come flocking to be
In prehistoric Roman Dorchester, all to see.
Dorchester, the only town in the world
Where history and learning could unfold
The wonder of Thomas Hardy,
that shy kindly man.
Why will Dorchester folk his genius ban?

———————

Fig. 25 The sign showing the
attractions of Dorchester,
removed in the 1970s?

Thomas Hardy's books and poetry are known world-wide. The countryside about which he writes and describes so vividly can still be traced and seen in all its beauty. The methods of farming a century and more ago and the people and customs of Dorset people can be seen in the County Museum.

5.9 Memories of Max Gate

When I had just started school in 1913 my eldest sister Gertrude took me for a walk to Max Gate. I was left outside. It was the year she played Marty South in Thomas Hardy's *The Woodlanders*. I was approached by a stranger who asked, "Does Thomas Hardy live in that house?" Evidently he must have been a Hardy enthusiast. I replied, "Yes, he does." At long last – to a child – my sister came to me to return to Dorchester. I told her about the stranger, then she said, "Didn't you tell him I was in there?" to which I replied "No, I didn't. Why should I?" Possibly this could have been my sister's first visit to Max Gate. Possibly she could have been very proud to have been invited there. She was sixteen years old then.

Of late years I have often found myself sitting in a very comfortable chair at Max Gate, Hardy's Dorchester home, where a rehearsal took place in front of Florence and Thomas Hardy just before the Hardy Players played '*Tess*' in 1924 at the Corn Exchange in Dorchester.

The first time, I wondered if more memories might arise. Many times I would tell visitors to Hardy's home about the rehearsal, emphasising Hardy's shyness and his understanding of human nature. For this reason a team of helpers would answer any questions regarding life at Max Gate during Hardy's lifetime. I met many interesting people of many nationalities, such as Japanese, American, German, Italian, French and Korean to name a few; all these because they recognised the genius of Thomas Hardy. For visitors to Max Gate to meet someone who had known Hardy personally usually proved to be a very unexpected experience for them.

Often I made them laugh for I would look up saying Hardy's words after he had written more on my script for me to say as Liza-Lu. He said "That's better isn't it?" with a twinkle in his eyes. He had already said he hadn't given Liza-Lu much to say, which was quite true.

On one occasion I was sitting on a comfortable seat in front of the fire at Max Gate, when the door opened and a crowd of Hardy Society members came into the room all talking at once in a crescendo of noise, getting louder and louder. I experienced pain in my head getting more intense every minute. I glanced towards the alcove in which the Hardys sat when 'Tess' was played before them in 1924. Did I see two grey figures there or was it imagination?

The pain in my head certainly was not imagination; it had increased and I shut my eyes temporarily. Looking in the same direction again all was normal. Did I imagine it or did it really happen? I shall never know, yet I know I do not normally suffer from headaches.

At a garden party at Max gate I was delighted to find that visitors could go upstairs to be shown the room in which the first Mrs. Hardy (Emma) spent the last years of her life, attended by a servant. Today her illness would be called dementia. After mounting the somewhat steep steps to this bedroom a small group of people listened to the guide explaining all that she knew of Emma Hardy. Her death caused her husband to write poetry which only those who have lost a spouse can really understand. I can.

Somewhat absentmindedly I said I did not like Mrs. Hardy, meaning Florence, his second wife. An excited female voice came nearer to say "You knew Thomas Hardy? Oh! it is wonderful for us to be here. Can I take a photograph please?" Two Japanese girls were gazing at me pleading for a photograph. How could I refuse? After that ordeal they very politely thanked me, bowing deeply to the ground as only the Japanese can.

I received through the post a Valentine. The first ever; still wondering who?

Part Six: A New Millennium

6.1 A new pair of eyes

Just before the old hospital in Princes Street, Dorchester had ceased to function, I paid many visits to Somerleigh Court, then the eye department of the hospital. At last I was ready for the operation to remove the cataract from the right eye. I told them I did not want to be put to sleep during the operation – I wanted to know what was happening. It was almost as though I were going to a theatre instead of a hospital judging by the people who were coming in, all talking to each other. The nurse held my hand and told me to press hers if I was worried about anything. Then the surgeon, I wasn't able to see him as he stood behind my head, kept saying "I can't get it". Each time he said this I felt a tiny tug on the eye ball. All of a sudden his voice changed, another tiny tug to the words "I've got it" and the operation ended. The surgeon afterwards congratulated me for keeping so still for such a long time. He added "That operation took one and a half hours. It usually takes three quarters of an hour". I think he was of Indian nationality, a wonderful surgeon. I had to stay in hospital for a few days. Later, when the new hospital had been built, I was summoned there to have an operation on my left eye, again a cataract. There was no comparison with the previous operation of some five years previously. This one was by laser. At the time I wrote a little poem about this operation which various church magazines asked permission to print. Here it is:-

The Operation

We entered the Hospital, I wasn't at ease
Oh dearie me, if I should sneeze.
Hungry was I, after six hours without food
But over such things I did not brood.
Others were there, long before eight
Sitting in rows awaiting their fate.
At last my turn came, the surgeon danced in
A poor sheep to the slaughter I saw in him.
The bed was high for my little short legs.
Up I went on it, after a push I begged.
Three quarters of an hour to keep quite still.
Five minutes it seemed did I go through the mill.
Of course I did not, I felt not a thing
I felt that a little song I could sing.
Pity I had no more eyes to be done –

That was to be the theme of my song.
Almost at once, I could see, oh, so clear
That marmalade, toast and tea which was so near.
I munched and munched and little thought
What joy to me that 'op had brought.
I can read small print without glasses now
To the silent laser beam I thankfully bow.

March 2000

It seemed strange to me to write a 2 instead of a 1, which I had always, throughout my life, been in the habit of doing. The year 2000, I have adjusted to it now.

2001 Dawns

The New Year dawns, an ominous grey;
I watched from my window, night steal to day.
Never have I seen over many long years
A dawn such as this; it filled me with fear.
A terrible red on the hilltop, no rim of sun,
The horrible grey of the sky, the day had begun.
Puffs of pink cloud came racing over the grey
Landscape, and then it seemed it was day.
The day it was with weird wind wailing so,
I felt so lonely, fearful, where could I go?
The oak trees, will they stand the force of the gale -
They have for years; but will their roots be tore
From the rain-soaked soil for ever more?
Their branches scream as at hurricane force,
The wind relentlessly takes its own course.
Slowly, so slowly, the wind ceased to be,
I looked from my window, my oak trees to see.
Sturdy they stand, they stand strong for me.

6.2 A visitor from Germany

One Thursday afternoon in August 2002, after I had returned from the Day Centre in Dorchester, I walked around to the back of the house to ascertain the amount of food the little wild birds had eaten from the various containers during my absence. Approaching the front door I noticed a stranger walking up the drive. He was about halfway when I called out "What do you want?" Actually I felt a wee bit frightened, only had a small watering can held in my hand if robbery was the motive. He stood still, then said "Are you Mrs Woodhall? I have come from Higher Bockhampton". That reassured me somewhat. He came nearer telling me he was very interested in the works of Thomas Hardy and he had understood that I knew him. I told him about the meeting – rehearsal rather – at Max Gate in 1924. Then he asked if he might take a photograph, the watering can was photographed as well. "How did you find out where I lived?" I asked. "The people in Owermoigne told me. They all seem to know you" he answered. The fact that he said he had been to Bockhampton first, I gathered that Owermoigne might have been mentioned. I noticed that he had a very slight foreign accent which did not seem French. Then I asked him. "I am a German" he said.

Fig. 26 The photograph that Hartmut Paulus took

Remembering two World Wars, and the one who had escaped to England from German occupation, caused me to show only too well that I did not like German people. He said "But that is long ago; Germany is a quite different country now". Rather belatedly I seemed to agree that it probably was so. I imagine he did not remember the last war. Then he thanked me and walked down to a waiting car.

Some time later I received a letter from Hartmut Paulus and the photograph he had taken of me, hoping I liked it. Now I know why he writes almost perfect English. He is a teacher of English and came to England some twenty years ago when he nearly contacted my sister Gertrude, but had to leave without being able to go to Beaminster. He has just realised that I am her sister. From one of his books on Hardy he quotes as follows:

> *'One of the few people whose presence invariably livened Hardy up in his eighties was Gertrude Bugler, the leading lady of the much loved Hardy Players. She shone in many dramatizations of his novels'.*

———

I imagine that is why, when he heard at Bockhampton that someone was still alive who knew Hardy, he went to such lengths to contact me. In his last letter, Christmas 2003 he writes that he hopes to be invited to my 100th birthday. He most certainly would be welcome should I be here to celebrate it.

6.3 A Hardy Society meeting

I had no intention of going to Stinsford Church on a freezing cold day in January 2003. A member of the Hardy Society persuaded me to go with her. I did not like to say no considering she had often taken me to Max Gate but I was more than apprehensive regarding the freezing cold weather. Actually I have never regretted going for I was to witness, with many others, one of the most beautiful, perhaps almost frightening sunsets I have ever seen. We arrived at Stinsford Church, the little church which holds so many memories for me, to sit in a seat near the pulpit. I had indicated that I would like to take part in the readings of Thomas Hardy's poems. I began to wonder if I could still throw my voice, as did all the Hardy Players, because the acoustics were so bad in the Corn Exchange at Dorchester. I chose *The Ruined Maid* to read, which Hardy wrote in the Dorset dialect. I seemed to feel that that little church must have heard a great deal of very broad Dorset dialect during the long years of its existence. I safely mounted the two or three steps up to the pulpit, placed my Hardy book of poems before me, then announced to the people present – *The Ruined Maid*.

Strangely, the mounting of the steps up to the pulpit threw my mind back to the dressing room in the Corn Exchange. A few steps there took the Players on to the stage. I seemed to go back in time, forgot I was in a pulpit – it became a stage temporarily to me, with an audience to be entertained. Instead of merely reciting the poem in broad Dorset dialect, I acted the two characters portrayed in it.

I came back to the present to hear prolonged loud clapping in a church. I was no longer in the Corn Exchange. Hastily I stepped down from the pulpit and returned to my seat to listen, or try to hear rather, some other members of the Hardy Society reading the poems of their choice.

Then it was time to view the Hardy graves in the churchyard. I turned to look back at the church. In the foreground the deep black shadowy shape of the church and the building opposite, between which the darkening sky could be seen. The sun had set, leaving behind the afterglow in a kaleidoscope of colour I find very difficult to portray. A camera could. Ominous purples with many shades of grey, lightened by a dull deep glowing red sky slowly sinking from my sight. A feeling of depression, almost a sense of horror descended on me. I seemed to be viewing nature in a very evil mood. I said to my companion "It's going to be a horribly cold night judging by that sunset." And it was.

We were afterwards entertained at a lovely old thatched cottage in a nearby Dorset village. Many times had I visited this village, but I had no idea that this cottage was there. A lovely warm inglenook fireplace with huge logs burning in it was a very welcome sight after looking at that menacing sky, and feeling so cold when in the churchyard.

The rest of 2003 proved to be a very busy and rather exciting year for me. I never knew what was going to happen next and a great deal did happen, very unexpectedly. I gave an illustrated talk on the Dorchester I lived in during my youth, to the Owermoigne Womens Institute. My husband had very painstakingly taken photographs of old prints of Dorchester, taking great interest while doing something at which he excelled. I incorporated two of Hardy's poems, one in the Dorset dialect, *The Ruined Maid*, which I partly acted as well. This my audience seemed to enjoy very much. The second poem, *The Voice* was received, as I hoped, in the silence it deserved. I think only those who have known bereavement can really understand or repeat that truly wonderful, deeply disturbing poem.

6.4 Bicycles

This talk helped me to make up my mind to approach the Curator of Dorchester Museum to see if a talk on the Hardy Players might be of interest. There seemed no doubt of that, the talk was booked for October. Meanwhile I was asked, because I knew Hardy, to give a little speech at Kingston Maurward to a group of cyclists attending an event called 'The Hardy Ride'. The group of cyclists numbered about 1500, some coming from France, Belgium and Holland as well as this country. The road I was taken along to reach Kingston Maurward was literally filled with cyclists. They were all across the road at times. It was a miracle there were no accidents. It was a very hot sunny day. On arriving I saw cyclists milling about haphazardly in all directions enjoying the freedom from traffic at Kingston Maurward. I indicated that I must not sit in direct sunlight having already dealt with two skin cancers. A seat was placed for me in the shade of a tree, listening to the local bell ringers, and overlooking the water in front of the house. My thoughts turned to my mother. How familiar this scene, albeit without the cyclists, would have been to her. Very near is the Elizabethan manor where her father's dairy was situated.

Eventually I was escorted into Kingston Maurward House to make my speech from the balcony. I can't remember what I said. I felt rather overwhelmed

Fig. 27 Myself being interviewed at Kingston Maurward when hundreds of cyclists visited the area to take part in 'The Hardy Ride' in 2003

at the dense mass of people in front of me and the cool mass of water in the background. However, what I did say pleased them. A lovely bouquet of flowers was presented to me and the ordeal was over. I retired into the large room with the lovely embossed ceiling. The journey home was accompanied by many cyclists occupying most of the road. It was a happy, very hot, sunny summer day.

6.5 On television

In July 2003 happened an even stranger occurrence! I found myself opening my solid oak door, originally sited in the demolished Abbotsbury mansion, to a television team. Such a camera I had never seen. I asked in amazement how much it cost? "About £5000" was the reply. "Fancy all that money walking into my home" I said, with a twinkle in my eye. This remark seemed very funny to the three operators; thus we became at ease with each other. They proceeded to move my furniture to their requirements then sat me in a position favourable to lighting possibilities and the producer started talking to me, asking various questions about Thomas Hardy. I spoke of the rehearsal held at Max Gate in 1924. This was easy for me. Many, many times I had repeated it to visitors at Max Gate. As they were leaving I noticed a very old looking bicycle strapped to the back of the car. They told me it was being used in the film. I recognised it when viewing the film before it was released to the public, at the Magistrates Court in Dorchester.

The next day the 'phone rang. "Do you have a photo of yourself when young, preferably at the time of the Hardy Plays?" I said "Yes, but it's the only one I have, and it's in a frame". I would not risk it through the post; lost letters were only too familiar to me. Arrangements were made for someone to fetch and return to me this photograph. It was included in the film.

A friend brought me a newspaper report on this television item shown on BBC 2. The report was on 13th August 2003, ending with these words:

> *"Either way, the programme was comprehensively stolen by 97 year old Norrie Woodhall, who knew Hardy when she was a young woman. "People didn't like him because he was an agnostic" she chuckled, "and so am I". She also recalled how kind he was to her – although a photograph showing what a stunner she'd been back then suggested that the great man's motives might have been mixed."*

The last line is absolutely untrue.

I remember writing a strong protest to the same paper just after my sister Gertrude's death in 1992 when similar, if not worse, insinuations were printed. My letter was ignored. That is why I have done my best to avoid publicity and the press till now. Now I feel it can only be through the press that hopefully Dorchester Councillors might see the future of Dorchester, the County Town, which should advertise the treasures it contains, unequalled by any other town in the whole world.

A lecturer on Hardy asked me to repeat *The Ruined Maid* in Dorchester at the museum after his lecture. After doing so I was escorted to the entrance of the museum by friends who were to drive me home to Owermoigne. A voice from the darkness reached me saying how much he had enjoyed The Ruined Maid. "It was worth coming to hear that." I was completely taken by surprise, but managed to say "Did you understand the Dorset Dialect?" "No, I didn't," he replied "but I liked the way you did it."

That was a great help to me, for I was already dreading the thought of my forthcoming talk at the museum. That day arrived all too soon. We arrived at the museum at about 4 pm. The weather favoured us fortunately. Of much interest was the watching of the preparations for the talk. I was given a seat on the little stage, thus could see everything. Chairs to be placed in rows, cameras to be set up, a screen nearby for me to manipulate at will, a hive of activity to get it all ready for 6.30 pm.

At first I thought I was to face a very small audience, just one or two people came in to choose their seats, then all of a sudden it seemed to me, all the seats were occupied. I started speaking to my audience sitting in my chair, then I meant to stand to recite *The Ruined Maid*. I nearly overbalanced because I had been motionless for such a long time. *The Ruined Maid* was, without doubt, ruined. I hastily sat down on my seat to give the audience the second poem intended as a direct contrast to the first, The Voice. The silence afterwards was as I had hoped. I knew then that I had 'got over' to my audience once again.

I produced my 1908 edition of *Under the Greenwood Tree*. From it I relived one of the scenes which was acted in the Corn Exchange in 1918, in the Dorset dialect. In 1918 the adaptation from the book to the stage was called *The Mellstock Quire*.

Someone in the audience called out "What about Lawrence?" [of Arabia]. I said "Yes, he came to one performance. I saw him looking across the empty stage, wondered who he was because he had such deep blue eyes. He was looking as if he would rather be elsewhere!" That certainly raised a laugh. Various questions were asked which I had no difficulty in answering, and to my great relief I had to talk no more. Again I was presented with a lovely bouquet of flowers. Of late I have read this criticism of that event: 'It was a remarkable performance for a woman who is nearly 100 years old'. Well, all I can think of to say is, I was very glad 'that woman' did not disgrace herself by falling to the ground, even if she ruined '*The Maid*'.

6.6 Three letters from the past

As I have said before 'truth is stranger than fiction'. I firmly believe that it is. So much has happened in my life to prove this. On the last day of August 2004 a visible link with the year 1914, and before that, became known to me. My niece Diana brought to me some letters she had found when sorting out a drawer containing many letters written by my sister Gertrude. She brought three, wondering whether I knew or remembered anything about them. I most certainly did – all of them. So many memories came flooding back.

In the first letter, I recognised the writing immediately. There was no signature of Reggie Barrow immediately. He was one of the Hardy Players who helped to form a concert party called 'The Gypsies' in 1914. I have many memories of him. He was quite a small man, so friendly, so sensitive regarding his lack of stature, a very clever unassuming gentle man. He wrote the appropriate words introducing each 'Gypsy' to the audience, set to the then very popular Negro song *Polly Wolly Doodle*. This introduction was always well received by the many audiences. When the Hardy Players repeated *The Mellstock Quire* in 1918 his rendering of Mr. Penny caused much hilarity in the audience. Physically he was Mr. Penny – 'a little small man' – Thomas Hardy's description, found in *Under the Greenwood Tree* from which *The Mellstock Quire* was adapted for the stage.

The play retained the exact words of the book; the two players were physically perfect for the parts. My sister Eileen played the part of Mrs. Penny. She was, to say the least, quite big for her age and rather too fat, suiting the part of Mrs. Penny very well indeed. The scene in Hardy's imagination takes place at a party in one of the many thatched cottages of those times around Bockhampton:

> 'The dance ended. "Piph - h - h - h!" said Tranter Dewey blowing out his breath in the finest stream of vapour that a man's lips could form, "a regular tightener thick 'un me sonnies!" He wiped his forehead and went to the cider mug on the table.
>
> "Well", said Mrs. Penny, flopping into a chair, "me heart haven't been in such a thumping state of uproar since I used to sit up on old Midsummer's eve to see who my husband was going to be".
>
> "And that's getting on for a good few years ago now from what I've heard you tell" said the tranter without lifting his eyes from the cup he was filling. Being now engaged in the business of handing around refreshments, he was warranted in keeping his coat off still, though the other heavy men had resumed theirs.
>
> "And a thing I never expected would come to pass, if you'll

believe me, cam to pass then", continued Mrs. Penny. "Ah, the first spirit ever I see on a Midsummer-eve was a puzzle to I when he appeared, a hard puzzle, so say I!"

"So I should have imagined; as far as that goes" said Elias Spinks.

"Yes" said Mrs. Penny throwing her glance into past times, and talking on in a running tone of complacent abstractism, as if a listener were not a necessity. "Yes, never was I in such a taking as on that Midsummer-eve! I sat up, determined to see if John Wildway was going to marry me or no. I put the bread and cheese and cider quite ready, as the witch's book ordered and I opened the door, and waited till the clock struck twelve, my nerves still alive, and so distinct that I could feel every one of 'en twitching like bell wires. Yes sure!, and when the clock had struck, lo and behold, I could see through the door a 'little small' man in the lane wi' a shoemaker's apron on".

At this point Mr. Penny stealthily enlarged himself half an inch. "Now, John Wildway", Mrs. Penny continued, "who courted I at this time, was a shoemaker, you see, but he was a very fair-sized man, and I couldn't believe that any such a little man had anything to do wi' I, as any body might. But on he came, and crossed the threshold – not John, but actually the same little small man in the shoemaker's apron . . .". "You needn't be so mighty particular about little and small!" said her husband, pecking the air with his nose.

"In he walks, and down he sits, and O my goodness me, didn't I flee upstairs, body and soul hardly hanging together! Well, to cut a long story short, by-long and by-late, John Wildway and I had a miff and parted; and lo and behold, the coming man came! Penny asked me if I'd go snacks with him, and afore I knew what I was about a'most the thing was done". "I've fancied you never knew better in your life; but I may be mistaken", said Mr. Penny in a murmur.'

The second letter was not even in an envelope. It too was yellow with age:

'To Arthur, from his sister Kate wishing him Many Happy Returns of his birthday, 11th April 1893.

PS: Now you are come to a man's age I thought I had better give my eldest brother, the 'son and heir', a little present suitable for a Christmas box. Of course, my present won't be half as nice as Gussie's *but I thought it would be better than nothing. Birthday Greetings and a kiss – old man . . . X'*

―――――――

Arthur was my father and Gussie (another Augusta) my mother. It was written by, to me, a very mysterious person my father would often refer to when looking at me saying "How like Kate you are". Then very sadly "poor Kate". He would never divulge anything to me about her. It seemed that he could not. She was someone he loved very much in the past. In those days I was not very interested so I never asked questions. It was not until towards the end of the last century that I was to know the truly sad story connected with Kate Stevens.

The third letter, addressed to Mr. Bugler, Woodbury House, Beaminster, had a green halfpenny stamp on which Dorchester is clearly marked. The envelope has a deep black edging. Inside the envelope, a card also with a black edging, 'In Loving Memory' on one side, with 'Henry Bugler, born 4th August 1833, fell asleep 4th April 1918' on the other. Underneath this in very small print 'With Christ which is far better'. On the opposite page, these words: 'Messrs. A H and H J Bugler and family express their thanks for all kind enquiries and sympathy'. This was, of course, the grandfather I had known and loved.

These three letters that have been brought to me have opened a flood of memories which had eluded me – memories of the 'Gypsies'; the excitement of being made-up – that is, a little more colouring added to my face; being taken to various places of entertainment after school hours to appear in front of an appreciative audience; the rehearsals. Such an exciting life for a child.

There was one thing that I did not enjoy very much. After giving a show, the 'Gypsies' often mingled with the audience. A soldier held me on his knee, his arms around me. I was not used to this and I struggled to get free. No doubt the soldier had children of his own, and probably endured the horrors of the battlefield later.

6.7 More letters from Germany

I received another letter from Germany, from Hartmut Paulus who came unexpectedly to my home in 2002. He suggests that there should be a revival of the Hardy Players – just like the rebuilding of the Globe Theatre in London, where Shakespeare's plays are again performed with great success. I rather think he has forgotten that Dorchester is somewhat smaller than London. He said that he intends to return to Dorset to be there, in 2005, when I celebrate my one hundredth birthday.

It turns out that Hartmut is a 'Friend of Shakespear's Globe' and a life member of the 'Friends of St. Paul's Cathedral'. He was instrumental in me receiving a birthday card from the Queen as he had written to His Royal Highness The Prince of Wales giving some information about my life.

In another letter he tells of how he came to know me. He wrote:

'As a pupil I had already read most of Thomas Hardy's novels. By sheer coincidence, I got a text by Thomas Hardy in my A-level exams. The result was so good that my English teacher never believed that I had not been cheating. But it was not until 1982 that I was able to visit Thomas Hardy country. With 'Tess of the D'Urbervilles' in my hands I visited many of the places mentioned in my favourite book, always trying to imagine how the heroine must have felt. I had all the symptoms of being in love with Tess. At the end of the day I wanted to see Hardy's birthplace. It was then 'guarded' by two elderly ladies, who did not charge you anything but insisted on showing you round by appointment only. So I had come all the way from Germany only to find Higher Bockhampton inaccessible. Finally, an act of prostration by myself and an English friend, a music teacher from Sussex, melted their hearts. They probably could not bear the thought of making two young men unhappy. Later I learned that we had been very lucky. Had we come during the Wimbledon fortnight, we would not have stood any chance whatsoever with the two tennis addicts. When leaving Hardy's birthplace, I asked them if there was still someone alive who knew the novelist. To my great surprise they said there was a lady living not far away. Unfortunately, we had to go back to Sussex that evening so we could not go and see her. For the next twenty years the thought that I had missed the chance of my life haunted me. In 2002 I came to Dorset again, this time with my wife. At the end of the 'Tess of the D'Urbervilles' tour we went to Hardy's birthplace. Now everything was

well organized, you had to pay an entrance fee and there were regular opening hours – fortunately no prostration necessary. I asked the same question again I had asked twenty years before – a rhetorical one I thought. This time I wasted no time. Having dropped my wife opposite Durdle Door – she was after some sunshine for a change, I went to Owermoigne and had a feeling of my life having come full circle.'

The ladies at Higher Bockhampton could have been referring to my sister Gertrude, rather than myself, who was living at Beaminster then.

Fig. 28   Gertrude Bugler, late 1980s

6.8 Stafford House

It all seems like a dream – a dream that could materialise in the near future. On 14th October 2004 I was taken to Stafford House to meet the new owners, an actor and his wife. He is also a screen-play writer and is well known in television. They could hardly believe that someone was alive who had known Thomas Hardy.

Stafford House was built around 1600, a beautiful grey stone building situated near the River Frome with many trees around, and kingfishers which, I told the owners, I have never seen in real life. The grounds are a wonderful little part of Dorset, not usually to be seen. After a welcome cup of tea and making friends with the little dogs I was shown the room where Thomas Hardy wrote some of his short stories.

I was asked whether I felt able to walk to the summer house. I saw a little gravel path which seemed a very long one to me. Then haltingly I said that I would try to do so; and I did. At the end of the path was a narrow wooden bridge which, it seemed to me, could be a hazard. Thankfully I managed to cross the bridge without falling into the river to be shown the summer house where, it was suggested, *The Return of the Native* could be performed in July 2005. I wondered about the comfort of the audience if midges decided to attack due to the nearness of the trees and river? That would be solved by hanging lanterns in the trees.

So it was decided by all concerned to put on the play, for an invited audience only. The proceeds would be donated to Cancer Care Dorchester. Later the play was to be put on in Dorchester and some of the villages, including Owermoigne.

Part Seven: Up to date – 2005

7.1 Reminiscing

Some thoughts having now reached the year in which I am to be 100 years old. Because I am physically in excellent health I do not feel at all old. I can see my doctor's face record his amazement when a routine check is made regarding blood pressure. Actually he did suggest that he did not know how to treat me due to my age! Is it because I do not add salt to anything I eat, and that I do not like alcoholic drinks or smoking? My one infirmity is increasing deafness, but even that is no longer the disability it once was. Modern digital hearing instruments restore a great deal. I can hear the clocks ticking the hours away once more.

Looking back over the long years now gone for ever I wonder why? so often, why? In my lifetime there has been a revolution caused by wars through the long years. I have known of a quiet, peaceful existence. Hardly a car could be heard and no aeroplanes roaring across the sky. It is a world to which I sometimes wish I could return. Life was then so uncomplicated; no noisy farm machinery breaking the peace of the country lanes and fields, a peace beyond imagination in today's world. The bird song could be heard as well as the farm animals, the crowing of the cockerels with their hens walking free, the lowing of cattle, sometimes the noise of a wagon drawn by horses – all country sounds not heard today. And there were not so many human beings. It was a world that man had not abused with devices abhorrent to nature, a world unknown to the atom bomb or the suicidal maniacs induced by unknown methods. Now a world becoming more complicated so fast that I find myself quite unable to comprehend what is happening in it.

To shatter the peace of my early years the 1914-18 war descended on the world, and peace disappeared for ever. With each war ways to kill became more and more inhuman – more and more shattering in every sense of that word – to the wars governments have involved my country in against the wishes of the people.

And is nature now rebelling against all of Man's devious devices? This rising of the waters killing thousands in an earthquake of such appalling ferocity – is this a warning of things to come? I have observed during my long life that nature, if abused, can call up all her powers to retaliate in one form or another. Nature controls this world we live in, not Man.

Time, ever faster with every year as I become older, seems all too soon to change from winter to spring and on to another year. The years travel so fast now I have at times to resort to a newspaper to make sure I know which year I am living in. I rarely spend a day by myself; so many friends come to be with me, which is wonderful, considering, as I write I am almost a hundred years old.

There was, and I hope it won't be the last, another visit to Stinsford Church to a carol service at Christmas time. The church looked lovely as only country churches can. The singing of carols, the whole atmosphere. Yes, a country church is the right place to be. Although I must say I felt somewhat embarrassed when the lady vicar looked directly at me announcing to the congregation that I was there. Seemingly a well known character in my very old age!

Christmas

Christmas now comes all too soon.
Supermarkets aglitter, there is no room
To stand and look hoping to see
Some of the shoppers just like me
Who know not what or where to be.
I feel I'm in a strange country.

Time was when Christmas was quiet.
A little shop, in you go and buy it.
A simple present could give such fun
But all of that alas is gone.
Children today do they know how to play?
I fear they sit with television all day.
Or try worrying old folk so they say.

In my young days many years now gone
We made our own fun and our own song.
I cannot help thinking – what has gone wrong?

———————

In many ways I feel sorry for the children of today for they lack the freedom which I knew, and the family life. Many endure untold grief when their parents decide to part. When I was young parents rarely left their children to endure such unhappiness.

7.2 An evening in Dorchester

I was requested by the Dorchester Association to give a talk about my early memories of Dorchester. The talk took place on 18th February 2005. The time had been changed from 6.30 to 7.30 so some of the audience had a long wait in rather cold conditions.

A certain amount of research for this talk brought me into contact with a member of the recently formed Stinsford History Society. She was very helpful, sending me copies of photographs of the people who lived in the Manor House at Stinsford, a beautiful water colour painting as the Manor was at that time, and a picture of James Fellowes and his wife who lived at Kingston Maurward House from 1853 to 1910.

Also included was a family tree of Thomas Way, whose will caused such a terrible row in my family. I have often wondered why his will stated he was from Toller Pocorum when he must have been living in part of the Manor House at Stinsford. Records of the Way family show that they were farming at Toller Pocorum in the 1700s. In those days the eldest son would inherit the family farm. I think Thomas Way was a younger son, and was to be found a farming interest at Kingston Maurward.

At the meeting I commenced by reading to my audience about Stinsford and Kingston Maurward, after which I found I was recovering from an attack of stage fright. After that, my memory was all that I needed for describing the Dorchester of about 1910 and later. The sad story of my chicken 'Little' caused a lot of laughter. I had feared it might have been the reverse. I felt quite relieved.

My husband had assembled old photographs of Dorchester, taking a great interest in doing so. A very helpful friend and a keen photographer has photographed the present Dorchester from the same viewpoints as the old photographs. Now they give great interest to many people as they record a very changed Dorchester especially in South Street.

This talk was reported at length in a local newspaper on 3rd March, the heading being 'A Hundred Years Young'. In the article were two photographs selected from seemingly countless numbers of photos taken that evening. They are the best I have seen of myself yet.

But there were two mistakes in the report, quite serious ones. The first was that I had persuaded Thomas Hardy to write extra lines for me when playing the part of Liza-Lu when 'Tess' was rehearsed at Max Gate in 1924. It was Thomas Hardy who wrote those lines in, certainly not at my suggestion.

The second mistake was that I was a pupil of Dorchester Grammar School when I actually attended Beaminster Grammar School. Dorchester Grammar School was for boys only.

I asked a friend to telephone the newspaper about these inaccuracies which she did. Speaking on the telephone is becoming very difficult for me now that I am becoming increasingly deaf.

On 17th March this newspaper printed the headlines 'Hardy, the Kind Man I Knew' stating that several readers had written to say how much they had enjoyed reading about my talk to the Dorchester Association. Then the corrections were printed, stating that they were happy to put the record straight. This has somewhat restored my faith in newspaper reports.

Fig. 29   Some of the Bugler family at my 100th birthday party.
Standing left to right: Michael Toms (Diana's son); Christine O'Connor (Diana's daughter);
Petrina and Peter Stevens; Pat Toms (Michael's wife). Seated left to right: Bette Bugler (Derek's
wife); Rev. Canon Derek Bugler; myself; my niece Diana Toms.

7.3 The clock

I had thought to end my book, but circumstances have arisen which caused me to change my mind and to write of an experience which I never thought could come to me, a truly frightening and unforgettable nightmare – to be confronted by burglars in broad daylight.

It was a Tuesday morning late in June 2005. I was expecting my niece Diana at any minute. She drives from her home in Beaminster each week to go shopping in Dorchester with me where we enjoy a meal together, and then to Crossways to change my books at the library there and then on to Owermoigne to get my groceries. I was expecting her at any moment. The front door bell rang. "That's Di" I said to myself and went to the door and opened it, to be confronted by a very tall man who immediately pushed his way into my house saying he had come in answer to my letter regarding the clock, the selling of my grandfather clock. For the moment I felt very confused regarding the supposed letter; then I knew. He had come to rob me.

By this time I had been manoeuvred into the room where the clock stood. The robber took out of his pocket a wad of notes saying he would give me £250, and counted the notes out. He then asked me about the part which was not in the clock. I said I did not know where it was. I had no intention of letting him stay in the house while I looked for it, so he reduced the money to £200. He called the second robber in to dismantle the clock and to take it outside to be placed in a large white car which stood very close to the front door. The first robber then asked me to sign my name on an almost blank piece of paper. I did as requested but not my usual signature. They then started up the car and left quickly.

A few minutes later my niece drove up to the house. The shock that I had just experienced caused me to feel that I wanted no one to know about it. I shut the door of the room where the clock had been and said nothing of the robbery to my niece. She said later that she thought I looked tired, probably having not been able to sleep very well owing to the very hot nights that were being experienced at the time.

After the trip with Diana to Dorchester and Crossways we met a close friend in the Owermoigne village shop. I clung to her causing her to wonder if something was wrong but I told her how glad I was to see her looking rather better after her brother-in-law's death. I wanted to tell her about the robbery but I found it impossible then.

That evening I revealed the robbery when I telephoned friends in Owermoigne. I could not remember everything. Perhaps, fortunately, so much may be wiped out of my memory!

The police were very understanding and helpful. They contacted the people in the Village to find out whether a white car had been seen there early on Tuesday morning. They asked to take the money paid to me by the robber, hoping to find finger prints thereon.

My doctor came as soon as he could, helping me in every way possible. He told me that I had done the right thing at the time. My bank was informed about the situation in case of fraud.

I have always felt nervous of very tall men, maybe because I am five-foot nothing. Now that fear has intensified out of all reason.

7.4 The New Hardy Players

The year 2005, especially the month of July, was a very rewarding and busy one for me. It was decided, by The New Hardy Players, to produce *The Return of the Native*, an adaptation by Tim Laycock the well known actor and musician, in celebration of my 100th birthday.

The New Hardy Players approached Emma and Julian Kitchener-Fellowes, then newly resident at Stafford House, regarding the possibility of staging an open-air production in their grounds. This they very graciously agreed to, Mrs. K-F entering wholeheartedly into the organisation of the event. It was she who suggested that we use the island where she has a pergola that proved ideal for the musicians who played such an important part in the production. Mrs. K-F also designed the programme and invitations, provided the chairs and arranged the supper. She and members of her staff served the food for the supper after the play. Julian K-F placed a hundred lanterns in the ancient Turkey oak tree, one for each year of my life. This was Emma K-F's enchanting idea. Julian K-F, aided by his son Peregrine, was at the entrance to greet everyone who attended the play.

The evening arrived. The weather was warm and windless; a long walk – for me – to the 'theatre' situated right by the river Frome; a summer-house as a background where music could be heard; the stage just in front with the trees and scenery, a wonderful setting. Many chairs for the audience completed the picture. After the play, a light supper. An evening quite unforgettable.

Dorchester's Town Crier, Alistair Chisholm, was in the play. He made a splendid speech afterwards. All could certainly hear him. I was surprised that he revealed I had survived after a cancer operation. I was told later that quite a few people in the audience were being treated for the disease.

On 17th July *The Return of the Native* was repeated in the garden of The Old Rectory in Owermoigne, by kind permission of Lynne and Charles Sandham who put a great deal of effort into adapting the garden, importing hay bales for seating and erecting a changing tent. Here are some extracts from the programme:

> *'The first production of 'The Return of the Native', performed by the Hardy Players in the early 1920s, was overseen by Hardy himself and featured Gertrude Bugler in the role of Eustacia Vye. Since that time the extent of the Dorset heathland has been drastically reduced and only in a few precious places is it possible to appreciate the wildness and solitude of the old Egdon.*
>
> *'However, the power of the story remains and we are pleased and proud to be able to present this new production as a birthday present*

for Gertrude's sister Norrie Woodhall. Norrie saw the original performance and remembers Thomas Hardy and the Mummers vividly.

'We are fortunate that Hardy's own interest and deep knowledge of local history, folk customs and music-making allows us to be so accurate with the music, song and dance chosen for this production. All the songs and tunes you will hear are from the local traditions, and dance tunes such as 'Enrico' (Hardy's favourite), 'Dribbles of Brandy' and 'Soldier's Joy'. We are also delighted that members of Frome Valley Morris Mummers have joined the company to perform the Mummers' play. The costumes and style of performance are based closely on the Mummers' play in the original production.

'The New Hardy Players were formed from the group of actors who performed 'A Life in Rhyme', the story of William Barnes who was Thomas Hardy's friend and mentor. They have been joined by actors from other drama groups, including two professional actors, MaryLou Delaplanque and Jonathon Brook, who play the leading roles of Eustacia Vye and Clem Yeobright.'

A performance at Corfe Castle provided a very different setting for the play. Admission was free but a collection was made towards the Charity. The final performance at the United Church in Dorchester helped to make a total of £2800 for Cancer Care and a cheque was presented to Caroline Nickinson in the garden of the lovely Old Rectory in Owermoigne.

Quite by chance, a friend recently found a manuscript in one of our country libraries. She thought it might be of interest to me. To my amazement it was the stage script, written by Harry Tilley in longhand, with all stage directions, of *The Return of the Native* by Thomas Hardy. This was performed by the Hardy Players at the Corn Exchange, Dorchester in 1921 when I was still at school. Later the Hardy Players performed this play in London, my sister, Gertrude, playing Eustacia Vye. It was a great success.

Fig. 30 '*The New Hardy Players' dressed for a rehearsal of The Return of the Native, 8th July 2005 in the grounds of Stafford House.*

Fig. 31 A painting of Gertrude as Eustacia Vye (The Return of the Native) circa 1922

7.5 My One Hundredth Birthday

The eighteenth of December 2005 – a fine winter day. Fortunately no snow for my hundredth birthday and party. I received many birthday cards, very beautiful cards, one or two with just Christian names. I have been trying to think whoever wrote them ever since they arrived.

Three o'clock saw me dressed as an old woman of Hardy's day and I quite successfully ascended the steps leading into the Village Hall of Owermoigne, to be there to receive my guests. Quite an ordeal.

One or two guests invited to the party I had not seen for several years and I could not remember what they looked like.

At about 4 o'clock the 'original' Hardy Player (myself) acted a short party scene of the late 1800s with two members of the New Hardy Players. Thus I had been able to write a playlet, and to play in it, using the exact wording from Hardy's *Under the Greenwood Tree*, and using my memory of 1918 when the Hardy Players performed *The Melstock Quire* adapted from Under the Greenwood Tree. And then, once again, I read *The Ruined Maid* in the Dorset dialect.

Fig. 32   The cast of the playlet enacted at my 100th birthday party
Left to right: Olive Blackburn, myself and Devina Symes

After that I read a short poem that I had written for the occasion:

A hundred year young today I be
Happy and healthy ye all can see;
Now if 'e do want to live as long as I
Baccy and drink 'e must seldom try;
Meat and three veg. They be good for you,
Some fruit as well. Now thick be true.
And now I must tell 'e, afore I forget
Thick be the best poem I've writ as yet!

I then felt thankful that the Dorchester Town Crier became the Master of Ceremonies, as it were. He remembered to say all that I had asked him to say and he made a striking picture in his Town Crier's apparel. He had written this poem for me on the occasion of my 100th birthday and he read it aloud:

Oyez Oyez Oyez
One hundred years ago today Norrie was born in Dorch..
For the County Town and its famous Son she proudly carries a torch.
She played Liza to her sister's Tess
Together this pair were the century's best.
She's soldiered on through smooth and rough,
This nestletripe's proved she's really tough.
So here's to Norrie and her hundred years,
Now join with me and give three cheers.

My niece Diana then requested my presence at her party table so that a photograph of the family group could be taken. Rather reluctantly I left my little group of Players to be confronted by two of the folks that I could not remember. Petrina and Peter Stevens had come from Buckinghamshire, the two people responsible for the story of my auntie Kate about whom my father would only tell me that I was "very like Kate". And the two sisters responsible for unravelling the story of the 1904 will of Thomas Way were there too.

The Owermoigne Womens Institute organised the party and proudly led me to see my birthday cake made by a member. Another member, Jean Branch, had decorated it and I have the top in a glass case to keep. In coloured sugar she had made a wild garden. Primroses, daffodils, even a fox and a little brown hedgehog walking up the gravel path leading to a gate. Truly a work of art, so wonderful for me to be able to show it to those interested over the coming years.

I did not wish for birthday gifts but donations for the hospices instead. In fact over £600 pounds was donated by my party guests.

I had spoken to Diana wondering if she could by any chance produce a shawl for me to wear in the playlet. To my relief she could and brought a beautiful hand-made shawl with a history. Some 200 years ago a great-great uncle had a disease possibly now described as arthritis. He decided to go to Bath for a 'cure'. And there he crocheted my beautiful deep red shawl. How it had survived all those years, a little faded in parts, I have no idea.

For the family photograph somebody removed the white Victorian hat that I wore for the playlet. Later, when I looked for it at home, I got really worried as it had been loaned to me. Eventually I learned that it had been found by the person who had loaned it, to my great relief.

Prior to my birthday I received news from Germany. A letter arrived saying that more was to come. It surely did – a letter not to be opened until 18th December. As the 18th was a Sunday, knowing I would have little time to remember to open letters, I'm afraid I disobeyed. I opened the letter a day early. Just as well, there being no delivery of letters on Sundays. Here were the contents

Fig. 33   My 100th birthday cake, made by the ladies of the WI and decorated by Jean Branch

of a letter written to Clarence House by Hartmut Paulus dated 4th September 2005, and on the Saturday before my birthday I received a beautiful birthday card from the Queen, a lovely photograph of her in colour with birthday greetings.

Hartmut would have liked to come to my party but was not able to do so because schools in Germany had not closed for the Christmas holiday. He also sent a birthday card, much larger than any other I had received, carefully packed each side with card for protection, with birthday greetings in German.

A friend has translated the card for me and this is what is written on this very lovely birthday card:

'For a Hundredth Birthday, Congratulations,
sent from Hartmut Paulus of Germany
to lovely Dorset, especially Lulworth Cove;
to Thomas Hardy's romances, especially
"Tess of the d'Urbervilles".
When a scholar I dreamt of speaking to someone who knew
Thomas Hardy personally. This dream is coming true
and for that I am very grateful.
My Family and I congratulate you, Norrie Woodhall, wholeheartedly.
Schmallenberg, Dec. 2005'

———————

As I write, tomorrow will be 6th January – Twelfth Night – when I will see all of my birthday and Christmas cards disappearing from my two rooms that they have decorated throughout the holiday. I shall miss them.

I have been reminded that I am living in my second century. What a thought. Why have I lived so long? And to have such a host of wonderful friends, all so much younger than I. Maybe it's because I have learned how to make people laugh, as well as being able to help some by quietly listening to what they have to say.

I should not boast too much about my health should I? One hundred years gone, no common cold this year or last, rarely a sleepless night. There was one – the night of my party. Yes, no sleep then!

I am looked after by a very caring doctor, who once told me that he did not know how to treat me, meaning my age.

Shall I live to see a world at peace, or shall I witness even more horrible devices to kill mankind and to eventually destroy this Earth on which I now live?

7.6 A diary from the past – and more

A few days after my 100th birthday my nephew Derek gave me the one personal present that I received, an unexpected one, and one which has given me enormous pleasure. It is a beautifully bound album containing many pages from my grandfather Bugler's diary, hand-written during the years 1911 to 1917 (when he was aged between 76 and 82). This diary once again was found at Beaminster. It makes very interesting reading proving, maybe, my memory of the past to be correct.

I shall now share some of his diary with those of you reading my story. This is the introduction:

Diary of Henry Bugler
resident of Dorchester
1835 to 1918
covering the years 1911 to 1917

Transcribed by The Reverend Canon Derek Bugler,
great grandson of Henry Bugler,
grandson of Arthur Bugler of No. 44 South Street Dorchester,
son of Arthur Thomas Bugler,
cousin of Diana Bugler of Beaminster
and
nephew of Augusta (Little Gussie) of Owermoigne
who is celebrating her hundredth birthday this month,
December 2005.

There is a photograph of my grandfather and another photograph of the six brothers (the youngest of whom is my grandfather) with their father. They all look very serious as they probably had to sit still for some time to have their photograph taken.

My grandfather notes everyday happenings as well as some of the things he had read and seemingly wished to remember. The diary contains references to various relatives coming to visit my much loved grandfather. I have chosen parts of it which I think might be of interest regarding life in Dorchester during the First World War.

On page 4 of his diary he writes:

'a charter was presented to King John which he unhesitantly
signed. This Great Charter or Magna Carta contained the foundation

of the Liberties of England. In short this Great Charter established the Government of England to be a Limited Monarchy. After signing the Charter King John sent to the Pope for Counsel etc. etc..

The Foundation of English Liberty Chapter XX 1199 – 1218.

It means checking the despotic power of the Monarch.'

On page 6 he writes that he paid a Mr. Burden for repairing boots 5/6d (approximately 28p).

On page 8: '*The Druids acted as priests of the Britons*'

'Saturday evening 7 pm. 17th February 1912. '*Miss Gertrude Mary Bugler came.*' She was to become his housekeeper. An unknown Londoner, out of the kindness of his heart, my grandfather gave her a home not knowing that she was an alcoholic.

'*From the Social Gazette Saturday April 6th 1912; Why we keep Easter. Our Anglo-Saxon Forefathers had a goddess called Ostara, in whose honour seasonal revels were held. The Saxon word Oster means rising and from this it is supposed we have derived the word Easter at which period we see in nature the resurrection of things. Easter is a Moveable Feast celebrated according to the time of the New Moon and this takes us back to the time of the Apostles. It is pretty clear that the Sanctity of Special Seasons was not in the minds of the early Christians.'*

On 3rd May my grandfather '*paid Mr. C Lock for a ton of coal. Paid him near the Brewery in Weymouth Road. Paid £1-1-0 when I told him that I bought the coal before the strike and raise in price.'*

Grandfather writes of the many relatives coming to visit him, the time of arrival and departure by train.

'*From the Social Gazette 14th December 1912: The White Slave Traffic – A glaring anomaly. Stated by Commissioner Cox at the City Temple. Shameful evil impeached. Not from Beneath altogether. Satan has no compulsory power over us He can tempt, persuade, allure, but consent is ours where there is cause to be found. In yourself only: in your yielding to outside influences. In the Parable of the Sower the Saviour tells us that some seed fell on thorny ground and the thorns sprung up and choked it. What are these thorns? The Saviour explains: the Cares of the World; the Deceitfulness of Riches, and the lusts of other things etc. etc..'*

1913

21st February, Friday: '*About the Suffragettes; agitation and hunger strikes. But through them the Government has shown curious lethargy in dealing with the situation. The recourse of legislation has not yet been exhausted. Ministers have been concerned to get their own Party measures through the House of Commons so as to ensure that they shall come under the provisions of the Parliament Act. That they have stood idly by, watching the law act as defiance by a small but determined body of militants. But Mr. Kenna's treatment of the Suffragette law-breakers had always been marred by weakness and vacillation.*'

27th March: '*We went to Strode Farm today. Mrs. A H Bugler*' (my mother) '*and her youngest daughter*' (myself) '*left Dorchester by the 9:08 GW train to Bridport. Left Bridport for Strode in a Victoria, and for the return journey. Came home from Bridport by the 8:32 train. Brought home a rabbit shot by William's son from Coventry at the farm*'.

All this was in grandfather's writing. This is something I have always remembered. I remember looking at the horse's rear, since I was sitting with the driver, and seeing the strain of the harness when the horse descended the quite steep hill leading to Strode Farm.

Sunday 6th July: '*44*' (No. 44 South Street) '*Gertie*' (my sister) '*near the lamp post talking to a young man and went out for a walk with him*'.

19th & 20th November: '*Hardy play.*' This was 'The Woodlanders' when Gertrude took the part of Marty South.

8th December: '*Hardy play in London. Mrs. A H Bugler*' (my mother) '*went up to mother her daughter, returned on Tuesday by late train*'.

1914

4th July: '*Arthur* (my father) *up in the bowling green when he ought to have been at 44 to help etc. etc..*' Several entries record my father playing bowls. I have memories of him with others playing in the Borough Gardens in Dorchester.

31st July: '*War news on the newspaper this day. Miss G Bugler went to the South Western Station and got a ¹/₂d paper this evening and read some of the war news.*'

11th August: '*I went up to the barracks to see the German prisoners but could not see them. A number of people there to try to see the German prisoners.*'

12th August, Wednesday: '*Eggs and poultry much cheaper today. Henry bought eggs at 10fi d per dozen, a great saving.*'

15th August: '*Crab brought up to me for breakfast.*'

24th August: '*Miss Gertrude* (my sister) *up early and in the bakehouse helping her father and brother.*'

5th September: '*Tom Young here and we had a job to get rid of him. Told*

Henry's wife not to send Tom with the newspaper as it was a job to get him away from here. Miss G M B (my auntie Gertrude) *complained of his behaviour to her, putting his hand where he ought not, etc. etc. and using bad language.'*

I remember Tom Young, a large hulking individual, decidedly 'simple', but not quite bad enough to be put in Herrison hospital.

23rd September, Wednesday: *'My nephew J W Bugler came to Dorchester and bought six young cock-birds and the following day went to Poundbury Fair. Returned in the evening.'*

8th October, Thursday: *'I went into Arthur's* (my father's) *garden and saw the poultry. Gussie* (myself) *up here for tea. She brought up flowers.'* This refers to the garden greenhouses and pig sty situated next to the Bowling Alley Walks, now of course built on in Trinity Street. But the old house once connected still stands.

The diary continues: *'Mrs. Bugler came up and told Miss G M Bugler about not letting her daughter Gertrude Amelia have sufficient clothes to keep her warm at night, and the mother went up into the bedroom and found more clothing when I was informed that there were nine blankets of mine. Miss G M Bugler got in a temper and went up in her bedroom. This is the second night of her going to bed first. Gertrude* (my sister) *has a bad cold.'*

19th October, Monday: *'London & South Western Railway special cheap excursion. Dorchester 8:24 am to Waterloo timed to arrive 12:18 pm. Miss G M Bugler went and returned on Thursday 22nd October, came here about 9:30 pm. Miss G A Bugler new housekeeper for four days.*

31st October: *'Miss G M Bugler paid for the S. Army ¹/₂d paper for 11 weeks including tonight 5¹/₂d.*

8th November, Sunday: *'Miss Gertrude Adelia Bugler of 44 South Street was confirmed in St. Peter's Church by the Bishop of Salisbury. The mother and little sister went to the church.'*

15th November: *'I forwarded 10/- by cheque to Princess Mary for the soldiers' Christmas Eve present.'*

8th December, Tuesday: *'I went down to 44 South Street. While there Gertrude Adelia came up to 3 Cedar Park Villa,* (his home) *could not find Gertie* (Mary). *She came back and told me. I came back to No. 3 when I found her at 3 Cedar Park and told her that Gertie* (Adelia) *had been up and could not find her. She said that she was upstairs but when I went up to No. 1 Princes Street* (where my uncle had his home) *I was told that she was seen running up the street in the rain toward the Plume* (the pub next door). *Gertie* (Adelia) *found that the door was not locked and no one in the house.'* By this time auntie Gertie seemingly was becoming suspected of her alcoholism.

18th December, Friday: '*Gertie and Queen (my sister Eileen) and Gussie* (myself) *had to go and perform before an audience at the Corn Exchange.*' This was by the 'Gypsies'.

1915

12th January, Tuesday: '*The young soldier was introduced to me. Gertrude and the young man went to Glastonbury.*' The soldier was Percival Alves who was later killed at Gallipoli.

10th March: '*Three more steamers submarined. "Princess Victoria" twenty miles off the Mersey Bar. The British steamer "Blackwood".*'

14th March, Sunday: '*25 soldiers had tea at No. 44 and on the 15th. I went out early to see them. They were in the Fair Field. [They] left for Plymouth and to East Africa. Had the front bedroom chimney swept, charged one shilling. Eggs offered at 9d per dozen in March and 8d per dozen in April and May. Both sons are thinking of liming eggs away for the winter.*'

3rd May, Monday: '*I went with Mr. Stovey to 14 Wollaston Road* (a property he owned) *and saw the door and the four windows and the stack pipe and the water roofing pipe etc.. Likewise the gate and railings to have one coat of paint and the door to have the old paint burned off and two coats of paint and grained and varnished. The four windows and stack pipe to have two coats of paint likewise, the roof water pipe and inside also. To cost 35/- .*'

20th May: '*Dorchester Sheep Fair.*'

9th June: '*I gave Miss Gertrude Mary Bugler a month's notice a little before 12 o'clock, when I told her that I intended to make a change after she was gone from here. I paid her £1-7-0 for the past month's wages due on the ninth. She asked me for 2/- when I paid for the month.*'

21st June, Monday: '*Gertrude up with us for tea, and Gussie (myself). Gussie brought up a pudding or raisin cake. Not very good. More German prisoners came to Dorchester; very rough most of them, so Gertrude said.*'

3rd July, Saturday: '*Gertrude cooked the loin of lamb and kept it in the oven too long and burned it, nearly spoiled it. I was very sorry to see the joint so burned up. It cost 4/2.*'

8th July: '*Mr. Walter Aries came here this afternoon and took away his sister-in-law, Miss Gertrude Mary Bugler.*'

9th July: '*Gertie's first Duty Day as housekeeper etc. etc..*' This was my sister Gertrude's first day as housekeeper to her grandfather.

Miscellaneous business items were listed in the diary, one of much interest to me regarding a headstone: '*Paid Mr. T H Tilley for the headstone, lead lettering, etc. £12-7-0.*' Was this for his wife, or for Kate? Grandmother would not have allowed

Fig. 34   Kingston Manor House painted circa 1893 by Henry Moule

her husband to erect a stone in her lifetime, that is quite certain. Yet another mystery of those far-off times?

_____

The older I grow the more convinced I am that truth is far far stranger than fiction. So much more information has emerged about my unknown relatives of the Way family (my mother's side) now that I have attained one hundred years of age! Three months after receiving my grandfather Bugler's diary for 1911 to 1918 yet another revealing letter arrived for me.

In 2005 I attended an exhibition of photographs at the old Manor House at Stinsford put on by the Stinsford Historical Society. This was where my mother and her family lived, before mother was married. The letter was from a very helpful member of the Society. At the exhibition she had drawn my attention to many of the very interesting photographs of the people who had lived in Stinsford and the Manor House in days gone by. The letter contained some photographs of Kingston Maurward's owners back in the 1800s, as well as a copy of a lovely painting by Henry Moule of the old Manor House as it was then.

She wrote:

'Since I saw you at the exhibition I have been able to find your great- grandparents and lots of brothers and sisters for Thomas. Your grandparents were at Toller a long time before they moved to Kingston Maurward – all their children were born and grew up there. When they left Kingston Maurward they moved to Tyneham. They appear on the 1901 census for South Tyneham and staying with them on the day the census was taken was your sister Gertrude, aged 4. Thomas was 60 by then and was "living on his own means". All his daughters had married by then – at Stinsford Church.'

_____

She sent me the Way family tree, resulting from her enquiries. Great-grandfather Thomas Way was born in 1799 and married Susanna. The fifth of their nine children was my grandfather, another Thomas who married Anne. The fifth of their five children was my mother Augusta who married Arthur Henry Bugler in 1896 at Stinsford.

Also of great interest to me was a receipt she had sent me for accommodation at the Central Hotel, Dorchester by a relative of hers when he stayed there a year or so after the 1939-45 war. My brother Arthur was in charge of the 'Central' then.

Almost unbelievable are the changes from then to the present day – Tyneham. My husband and I loved to drive to Tynham when it was opened to the

Fig. 35   Autumn at Sunnybrook.

public. Little did I know then in the 1960s that Tynham was in any way connected with the Way family and my unknown grandfather. I always felt sad and depressed to see the ruined cottages, their inhabitants no longer there, only people who came to stare at the devastation everywhere. The lovely old Elizabethan manor house could not be seen. It no longer existed. It was once the home of the Bond family.

Monica Hutchins wrote *Inside Dorset* in 1965. I still have a copy. She loved Dorset and wrote a lot of books at this period. She organised a petition which was signed by many many people, ourselves included, to be presented to the War Department for the release of Tynham to its rightful owners – to no avail. Now beautiful and remote, Tyneham and Worbarrow Bay remain at the mercy of those who practise war conditions. Perhaps the wild flowers there will be able to increase.

7.7 The secrets of longevity

I found, inserted under my front door, from a near neighbour, a newspaper cutting, part of which is as follows:-

> *'People really do get older and wiser according to researchers who claim to have exposed the idea of a doddery old age as a myth. Their study shows that the fears many have about living into their nineties and beyond ending up frail and forgetful in a nursing home are largely unfounded. In fact, many of the 111 nonagenarians who took part in the research proved sharper and more quick witted than counterparts decades younger.'*

This really cheered me up, and I felt I could I without doubt tell those town councillors a thing or two about the prosperous Dorchester I remember, when Dorset people were in power on the councils.

Perhaps now is a good time to give my recipe for living. First of all, learn to relax – it took me years. Just sit comfortably, takes some deep breaths and try to forget everything. Think of the wonders of a wild garden and by then you'll have probably got to sleep, which is Nature's way of healing. There are times when I try to do too much. Mother Nature says 'do nothing, just forget everybody'. Sometimes, probably due to my age, I relax most of the day. The next day I find I can 'get up and go'. Don't get angry or cross with anyone. Blood pressure goes up which in my case used to give me a headache. At my age I can smile at anyone. And a smile often causes a smile in return. It does me good as well. You are what you eat. Plenty of vegetables with some meat, plus fresh fruit keeps me very fit. If there is anything on your mind, don't bottle it all up; choose someone you know you can trust to listen to you. By being able to speak about what is so worrying to you, you can relax the tension caused by keeping to yourself. I know this works as I have listened to many to enable them to help themselves. And above all – take no risks when driving a car!

7.8 Epilogue

If I could go back in time it would be to the world of my childhood, a quiet peaceful world that was all too soon to vanish for ever, a world in which children were seen and not heard. Maybe it was rather boring for children to have to sit with their parents and friends discussing the happenings which interested them. A great pity that I cannot remember the – to me – very boring subjects being discussed. They could have been about very interesting family history.

All my life I have lived close to nature and have been able to witness her in many moods. Sometimes she is very frightening. I have never been able to control my fear of lightning. Actually, I always feel quite ill during a thunderstorm. My husband likewise loved nature. A thunderstorm never upset him as he could hardly hear it. We loved watching the wild birds flying to the bird table. They could be quite aggressive towards each other at times. In the past there were many blue tits coming to the bird table. This year I have seen very few – indeed there are not so many birds to be seen at all. Are there too many birds of prey in the country?

The World To Be

This wonderful world, now so defiled
By Man's greed, so horribly spoiled,
Where will it all go, where will it all end?
Will Nature rebel and will Nature send
Waters from the north that world to end,
To receive as once it has before?
The ice age again, again temperatures soar
To create another world so quiet so clean
Which I saw in my childhood, or was it a dream?

There were no cars, no planes to roar;
Little dusty lanes – yes eyes were sore,
Just a wonderful silence. Did I hear
The hum of the bees from hives so near,
The crowing at dawn of cockerels bright
Later to challenge each other to fight,
The gentle lowing of cattle come from afar,
The pigs in a field grunting and the lambs bah bah,
The country sounds as once they were.

Few there are now left even to care.
The countryside now so seldom seen,
Fading fast to bricks, no longer green.
Will Mother Nature rear herself to say
"Enough of this, I'll now have my way,
Away with it all". The north ice swells,
Icebergs move towards lake and dell,
Melting, cascading o'er land and sea,
And the land, the land, not to be?

The End

List of Figures